LISTENING TO VAN MORRISON

Greil Marcus is the author of *Bob Dylan: Writings 1968–2010*, *Like a Rolling Stone*, *The Old, Weird America*, *The Shape of Things to Come*, *Mystery Train*, *Dead Elvis*, *In the Fascist Bathroom* and other books. A twentieth anniversary edition of his *Lipstick Traces* was published in 2011. With Werner Sollors, he is editor of *A New Literary History of America*, published by Harvard University Press. Since 2000, he has taught at Princeton, Berkeley, Minnesota, and the New School in New York. His column "Real Life Rock Top 10" appears regularly in *The Believer*. He lives in Berkeley.

Further praise for *Listening to Van Morrison*:

'More a series of non-fiction short stories than a straight-forward analysis. Marcus devotes virtually every chapter to a wide-ranging discussion of a Morrison album, song or live performance. Fittingly, just as the singer peppers his songs with eclectic allusions to Muddy Waters and William Blake, Marcus, too, brings in endless cultural signifiers, the better for us to understand the music.' Peter Gerstenzang, *New York Times*

LISTENING TO
VAN MORRISON

GREIL MARCUS

faber and faber

First published in 2010
by Faber and Faber Limited
Bloomsbury House, 74–77 Great Russell Street
London WC1B 3DA
This paperback edition first published in 2012

Printed in England by CPI Group (UK) Ltd, Croydon CRO 4YY

"It's All in the Game" lyrics by Carl Sigman,
music by Charles Gates Dawes. Copyright © 1951 (renewed) by
Music Sales Corporation. International copyright secured.
All rights reserved. Used by permission.

Designed by Trish Wilkinson

A CIP record for this book
is available from the British Library

ISBN 978–0–571–25446–0

1 3 5 7 9 10 8 6 4 2

CONTENTS

PART THREE
A BELIEF IN THE BLUES AS A
KIND OF CURSE ONE PUTS ON ONESELF

PART FOUR
THERE WAS NO FALSE FACE THE SONG COULD NOT ERASE

For Dave Marsh

NORTHERN MUSE. GREEK THEATRE, BERKELEY.
3 MAY 2009

The fourteen-piece band assembled for a concert in which Van Morrison was to perform the whole of his forty-one-year-old album *Astral Weeks* so dominated the stage you might not have even noticed the figure seated at the piano; the sound Morrison made when he opened his mouth seemed to come out of nowhere. It was huge; it silenced everything around it, pulled every other sound around it into itself—Morrison's own fingers on the keys, the chatter in the crowd that was still going on because there was no announcement that anything was about to start, cars on the street, the ambient noise of the century-old open-air stone amphitheatre, where in 1903 President Theodore Roosevelt spoke, where in 1906 Sarah Bernhardt appeared to cheer on San Francisco as it dug out of its ruins, where in 1964 the student leader Mario Savio rose to speak to the whole of the university gathered in one place and was seized by police the instant he stood behind the podium as the crowd before him erupted in screams, where Senator Robert F. Kennedy spoke in 1968, days before he was shot. The first word out of Morrison's mouth that night, if it was a word, not just a sound, something between a shout and a moan, was, you could believe, as big as anything that ever happened on that stage.

INTRODUCTION

In 1956, the stiff and tired world of British pop music was turned upside down by Lonnie Donegan's "Rock Island Line," a skiffle version of a Lead Belly song, played on guitar, banjo, washboard, and homemade bass. Like thousands of other teenagers, John Lennon put together his own skiffle band in Liverpool that same year; Van Morrison, born George Ivan Morrison in 1945 in East Belfast, in Northern Ireland, formed the Sputniks in 1957, the year the Soviet Union put the first satellite into orbit and John Lennon met Paul McCartney. Morrison would never find such a comrade, and, unlike the Beatles, he would never find his identity in a group. Whether in Ireland, England, or the United States, he would always see himself as a castaway.

East Belfast was militantly Protestant, but Morrison's parents were freethinkers; even after his mother became a Jehovah's Witness for a time in the 1950s, his father remained a

committed atheist. The real church in the Morrison house-
hold was musical. There was always the radio ("My father was
listening to John McCormack"); more obsessively, there was
"my father's vast record collection," 78s and LPs by the all-
American Lead Belly, and within the kingdom of his vast
repertoire of blues, ballads, folk songs, protest songs, work
songs, and party tunes that dissolved all traditions of race or
place, the minstrel and bluesman Jimmie Rodgers, cowboy
singers of the likes of Eddy Arnold and Gene Autry, the bal-
ladeer Woody Guthrie, the hillbilly poet Hank Williams, the
songsters Sonny Terry and Brownie McGhee, the gospel blues
guitarist Sister Rosetta Tharpe—and later Muddy Waters,
Howlin' Wolf, Little Walter, John Lee Hooker, Big Joe Williams, all of them magical names. Thus when the thirteen-
year-old singer, guitar banger, and harmonica player Van
Morrison went from the Sputniks to Midnight Special, named
for one of Lead Belly's signature numbers—and after that
from Midnight Special to the Thunderbolts, a would-be rock
'n' roll outfit that tried to catch the thrills of Jerry Lee Lewis
and Little Richard, and from the Thunderbolts to the Mon-
archs Showband, a nine-man outfit with a horn section, cho-
reographed shuffles, and stage suits that would play your
company dinner, your Christmas party, your wedding, and
which in the early '60s toured Germany offering Ray Charles
imitations to homesick GIs, only a patch of the map Morrison carried inside himself had been scratched.

   In 1964, in Belfast, with the band Them, Morrison began
to find his style: the blues singer's marriage of emotional ex-
tremism and nihilistic reserve, the delicacy of a soul singer's
presentation of a bleeding heart, a folk singer's sense of the

uncanny in the commonplace, the rhythm and blues band-leader's commitment to drive, force, speed, and excitement above all. The group's name, calling up the 1954 horror movie about giant radioactive ants loose in the sewers of Los Angeles, was full of teenage menace:

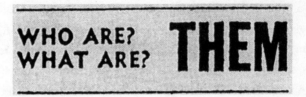

ran ads in the Belfast *Telegraph*. With Morrison pushing the combo through twenty minutes of his own "Gloria," night after night in the ballroom of a seamen's mission called the Maritime Hotel, Them began to live up to its name.

Cut to three minutes or less on 45s, the band's songs would soon bring Morrison a taste of fame. In 1965, in London—"Where," the liner notes to Them's second album quoted Morrison, "it all happens! . . ."—the group crumbled, but Morrison recorded under their name with a few members of the band and a clutch of studio musicians. Though Morrison would disavow them as the most paltry reductions of what had happened at the Maritime—"It wasn't even Them after Belfast," Morrison told me one afternoon in 1970, as he told others before and since—Them made two unforgettable albums, harsh in one moment, lyrical in the next. In 1965 and 1966 Them scored modest hits on both sides of the Atlantic: "Gloria" (covered by the Chicago band the Shadows of Knight, who had the bigger hit in the U.S.A., except on the West Coast), "Here Comes the Night," "Baby Please Don't Go," "Mystic Eyes."

To those who were listening, it was clear that Van Morrison was as intense and imaginative a performer as any to have emerged in the wake of the Beatles and the Rolling Stones—who, he claimed of the latter band in angry, drunken moments, stole it all from him, from *him*! Yet it was equally clear, to those who saw Them's shows in California in 1966—at the Fillmore Auditorium in San Francisco, and at the Whisky A-Go-Go in Los Angeles in 1966, where the group headlined over Captain Beefheart one week and the Doors the next—that Morrison lacked the flair for pop stardom possessed by clearly inferior singers, Keith Relf of the Yardbirds, Eric Burdon of the Animals, never mind Mick Jagger, who in those days were seizing America's airwaves like pirates, if not, as with Freddie and the Dreamers or Wayne Fontana and the Mindbenders, conning the nation's youth like the King and the Duke bamboozling Huck and Jim. Morrison communicated distance, not immediacy; bitterness, not celebration. His music had power, but too much subtlety for its power not to double back into fear, loss, fury, doubt.

What he lacked in glamour he made up in strangeness—or rather his strangeness made glamour impossible, and at the same time captivated some who felt strange themselves. Morrison never covered Randy Newman's "Have You Seen My Baby?"—"I'll talk to strangers, if I want to / 'Cause I'm a stranger, too"—he didn't have to. He was small and gloomy, a burly man with more black energy than he knew what to do with, the wrong guy to meet in a dark alley, or backstage on the wrong night. He didn't fit the maracas-shaking mode of the day. Instead, in 1965, he recorded a ghostly version of "It's All Over Now, Baby Blue" that outran Bob Dylan's original, and then turned the fey Paul Simon rewrite of Edward Arlington Robinson's 1897 poem "Richard Cory" into a bone-chilling fable of self-loathing and vengefulness.

In 1966 Morrison abandoned the last remnant of Them—its name—and put himself altogether under the wing of the legendary New York record man Bert Berns, renowned for writing or producing Solomon Burke's "Cry to Me," Erma Franklin's "Piece of My Heart," Garnett Mimms's "Cry Baby," and the Isley Brothers' "Twist and Shout," not to mention "Here Comes the Night." In 1967 they made the single "Brown-Eyed Girl," after which Berns, working from sometimes unfinished recordings, rushed out a dark, cracked-blues album called *Blowin' Your Mind!* (the phrase was already as out-of-date as the soupy psychedelic jacket); the signature number was the nearly ten-minute "T. B. Sheets," which was exactly what it was about. Who wanted to listen to an endless cynical number about a woman dying of tuberculosis, closer to a bilious stand-up routine than a song, when the air was filled with "San Francisco (Be Sure to Wear Flowers in Your Hair)"?

The bright, bouncy "Brown-Eyed Girl" was Morrison's least convincing recording and his first top-ten hit single—and, except for "Domino" in 1970, so far his last. Though "Brown-Eyed Girl" has stayed on the radio ever since, at the time Morrison himself was quickly forgotten; he had both trivialized himself and blown himself up. His career was all but destroyed. When Nik Cohn's *Pop from the Beginning*, the first good rock 'n' roll history, appeared in 1969, even when a revised edition came out in 1973, neither Them nor Morrison were even mentioned.

Consumed by resentment over the swindle of stardom, fame, records, money, debt, and oblivion, caught in a trap of performing and publishing contracts after Berns's death at the end of 1967, Morrison found himself in Boston, where late-night DJs soon got used to a character with an incomprehensible Irish accent drunkenly pestering them for John Lee Hooker music. One night Morrison was booed off the stage when Peter Wolf, then the leader of a local band called the Hallucinations, brought him out of the audience to front their version of "Gloria." "Don't you know who this is?" Wolf shouted at the hissing crowd. "This man *wrote the song*!" But they didn't know. In 1967, when you said Morrison you meant the Doors, who, one could have read at the time, were at work on "their new masterpiece": *their* version of "Gloria."

Morrison returned to Belfast, apparently a burnt-out victim of the pop wars. There he wrote a set of songs about childhood, initiation, sex, and death, which finally took form as *Astral Weeks*. It was as serious an album as could be imagined, but it soared like an old Drifters 45, "When My Little Girl Is Smiling" or "I Count the Tears." From there Morrison's music opened onto the road it has followed since: a road bordered by meadows alive with the promise of mystical deliverance and revelation on one side, forests of shrieking haunts and beckoning specters on the other, and rocks, baubles, traps, and snares down the middle. With his wife, he moved to the musicians' pastoral bohemia of Woodstock, then to the San Francisco Bay Area, celebrated a domestic paradise, and pledged to walk down Broadway in his hot pants. Then his paradise fell to pieces, and his music shot back and forth between false promises and affirmations too hard-won to deny, from upstate New York to Marin County under a Belfast cloud, idyll and civil war, inspiration and boredom, the platitudes of a New Age seeker and the bad news of someone convinced that no one is listening, down ten, twenty, thirty, forty years, by now almost half a century, to find a man now brooding in his present-day redoubt in Bath, dreamy site of Roman spas, John Wood's eighteenth-century Druidic power spot Bath Circus, and Morrison's own Exile Productions. "The only thing that matters is whether you've got it or not," he once said. "The only thing that counts is whether you're still around. I'm still around." Yes, and so what? As a physical fact, Morrison may have the richest and most expressive voice pop music has produced since Elvis Presley, and with a sense of himself as an artist that Elvis was always denied. But what is that voice for?

Van Morrison's music as I hear it holds a story—a story made of fragments. There is in his music from the very first a kind of quest: for the moment when the magic word, riff, note, or chord is found and everything is transformed. At any time a listener might think that he or she has felt it, even glimpsed it, a realm beyond ordinary expression, reaching

out as if to close your hand around such a moment, to grab
for its air, then opening your fist to find a butterfly in it—
but Morrison's sense of what that magic moment is must be
more contingent. For him this quest is about the deepening
of a style, the continuing task of constructing musical situations in which his voice can rise to its own form.

"When I was very young," the late Ralph J. Gleason
wrote in 1970 in a review of Morrison's album *Moondance*,
"I saw a film version of the life of John McCormack, the
Irish tenor, playing himself. In it he explained to his accompanist that the element necessary to mark the important
voice off from the other good ones was very specific. 'You
have to have,' he said, 'the yarragh in your voice'"—and to
get the yarragh, for Morrison, you may need a sense of the
song as a thing in itself, with its own brain, heart, lungs,
tongue, and ears. Its own desires, fears, will, and even ideas:
"The question might really be," as he once said, "is the song
singing you?" His music can be heard as an attempt to surrender to the yarragh, or to make it surrender to him;
to find the music it wants; to bury it; to dig it out of the
ground. The yarragh is his version of the art that has
touched him: of blues and jazz, for that matter of Yeats and
Lead Belly, the voice that strikes a note so exalted you can't
believe a mere human being is responsible for it, a note so
unfinished and unsatisfied you can understand why the
eternal seems to be riding on its back.

Morrison will take hold of the yarragh, or get close to it,
raise its specter even as he falls back before it, for the moment
defeated, with horns, volume, quiet, melody and rhythm and
the abandonment of both, in the twist of a phrase or the

dissolution of words into syllables and syllables into preverbal grunts and moans. He will pursue it perhaps most of all in repetition, railing or sailing the same sound ten, twenty, thirty times until it has taken his song where he wants it to go or failed to crack the wall around it. The yarragh is not, it seems, something Morrison can get at will, or that in any given year or even decade he is even looking for; the endless stream of dull and tired albums through the 1980s and '90s, carrying titles like warning labels—*Beautiful Vision*; *Poetic Champions Compose*; *Avalon Sunset*; *No Guru, No Method, No Teacher*; *Inarticulate Speech of the Heart*; *A Sense of Wonder*; *Enlightenment*—attest to that. So do a string of records where Morrison seems to attempt to reduce whatever might be elusive, undefinable, and sui generis in his music to parts that can never recombine into a whole, as he recorded jazz and jump blues with his sometime accompanist Georgie Fame, country with Linda Gail Lewis, Jerry Lee's sister, traditional Irish songs with the Chieftains, and, most touchingly, even skiffle with Lonnie Donegan himself, back in Belfast, two old men standing up to the crowd to sing "Midnight Special," not so far from where, once, one of them named a band after it. Those are episodes in a career. It's the fragments of music as broken and then remade by the yarragh that this book is looking for. "The only time I actually work with words," Morrison said in 1978, "is when I'm writing a song. After it's written, I release the words; and every time I'm singing, I'm singing syllables. I'm singing signs and phrases."

The quest for the yarragh—for moments of disruption, when effects can seem to have no cause, when the sense of an unrepeatable event is present, when what is taking place in a song seems to go beyond the limits of respectable speech—is also a performer's quest to evade and escape the expectations of his audience. It's a struggle to avoid being made irrelevant and redundant, a creature tied as if by chains to his hits of forty, thirty, twenty years earlier, even to the song that hit last month—forbidden, by the laws of the pop mind and the pop market, from ever saying anything he hasn't said before. The result is a distrust of the audience, coming out, on any given night, in anger, insult, drunkenness, disdain directed at the singer's own songs as much as toward whatever crowd might be present. From the time of his first hits Morrison has, in a way, set himself against any possible audience: he does his work in public, but with his back turned, sometimes literally so—and it might go back to those nights in the Maritime Hotel in 1964. "Out of nowhere, these kids began showing up," Morrison said in 1970, and I remember the way his eyes sparkled in a set, stolid face as he talked: "Sometimes, when it all worked, something would happen, and the audience and musicians would be as one." That was because no one knew what might happen—and no one knew what was supposed to happen. Before a song is recorded, there is no right way; afterward, especially in the pop glare, audiences know what to expect and expect what they know.

Van Morrison, then, is a bad-tempered, self-contradictory individual whose work is about freedom. How do you get it? What do you do with it? How do you find it when it disappears—and what is it? Is the yarragh the means to freedom, or is it, when you can find it, the thing itself? When Morrison reaches the moments of upheaval, reversal, revelation, and mirror-breaking that are this book's subject—in his music and, sometimes, in what other people have done with his music, finding, as Neil Jordan would do with Morrison's music in his film *Breakfast on Pluto*, a yarragh behind the yarragh, or dramatizing it as Morrison might not—all of those questions are thrown into relief.

It becomes plain that any summing up of Morrison's work would be a fraud. That is what makes his failures interesting and his successes incomplete; it's what allows the most valuable instances of his music to exist less in relation to other instances in his career in any historical sense than in a kind of continual present. It's that territory I will try to map.

Ralph J. Gleason, "Rhythm: A Young Irishman Haunted by Dreams," *San Francisco Chronicle*, 1 March 1970.

"My father was listening": interview with Dave Marsh, "Kick Out the Jams" (Sirius XM Radio, 8 March 2009).

"The only time": Jonathan Cott, "Van Morrison: The *Rolling Stone* Interview," *Rolling Stone*, 30 November 1978, 52.

Mario Savio's oratory can be heard on *Is Freedom Academic? A Documentary of the Free Speech Movement at the University of California at Berkeley* (KPFA-Pacifica Radio, LP, 1965). See also Robert Cohen, *Freedom's Orator* (New York: Oxford, 2009).

The Heart and Soul of Bert Berns (UMVD, 2002). Includes Berns's productions of "Everybody Needs Somebody to Love" and "Cry to Me" by Solomon Burke, "Cry Baby" by Garnett Mimms, "Piece of My Heart" by Erma Franklin, and "Twist and Shout" and "I Don't Want to Go On Without You" by the Isley Brothers. *The Bert Berns Story Volume 1: Twist and Shout 1960–1964* (Ace, 2008) features an end-of-the-journey-to-the-end-of-the-night composite photo of Solomon Burke and

Berns facing the abyss in the studio while Little Esther Phillips, in a gleaming white dress, looks on; it includes "A Little Bit of Soap" by the Jarmels, the obscure "If I Didn't Have a Dime (to Pay the Jukebox)" by Gene Pitney, "Gypsy" by Ben E. King, "Look Away" by Garnett Mimms, "Mojo Hannah" by Little Esther Phillips, "Killer Joe" by the Rocky Fellas, and "Here Comes the Night" by Lulu. *Sloopy II Music Presents the Songs of Bert Russell Berns* (B00, no date, but going for $399 on eBay) collects forty-four tracks on two CDs, including "Here Comes the Night" by both Them and (in his unhinged *PinUps* version) David Bowie, "Are You Lonely for Me Baby" by both Freddie Scott and Otis Redding & Carla Thomas, "Baby Come On Home" by Solomon Burke and Led Zeppelin, "Cry Baby" by Garnett Mimms and Janis Joplin, "Goodbye Baby (Baby Goodbye)" by Solomon Burke and Janis Joplin, "I Want Candy" by the Strangeloves and Bow Wow Wow, "Piece of My Heart" by Erma Franklin and Janis Joplin, and "Tell Him" and "Run Mascara Run" by the Exciters.

Van Morrison, *Blowin' Your Mind!* (Bang, 1967).

———*Astral Weeks* (Warner Bros.–Seven Arts, 1968).

PART ONE

A GRIMY CINDERELLA IN A PURPLE STAGE SUIT

MYSTIC EYES. 1965

It came barreling out of car radio speakers like a flood on a black night. Surrounded by some of the best and most tuneful pop music ever made—the Beach Boys' "I Get Around," Petula Clark's "Downtown," the Supremes' "Stop! In the Name of Love," Wilson Pickett's "In the Midnight Hour," the Beatles' "Eight Days a Week," the Miracles' "The Tracks of My Tears," Bob Dylan's "Like a Rolling Stone," Otis Redding's "I've Been Loving You too Long (to Stop Now)," the Byrds' "Turn! Turn! Turn!"—even up against Sam the Sham and the Pharaohs' "Wooly Bully"; even up against Them's own "Gloria" or "Here Comes the Night"—this made no sense. You couldn't see through it, you couldn't see into it. What was happening?

It starts in the middle, as if you've switched stations halfway through some other song without realizing it. It's moving so fast you feel as if you'll never catch up. The band—guitar, drums, bass, an organ hovering in the background—can't catch up with the harmonica that's leading the charge, Little Walter as a nightrider; suddenly they do, and then they take a step ahead. You realize that the last thing you want is for the harmonica—high, implacable, uncaring, a body without a mind, it seems to be its own force, not some mere instrument played by some particular person who has to get up in the morning and go to sleep at night—to lose this race. It doesn't; it cuts in front of the stampeding combo, playing a swirling pattern that focuses the band. There's a call and response, a joining of forces, no longer one against the others, but a whole against a part, and the part is whoever's listening. You're the target. You're about to be left behind, to the wasteland this flood will leave in its wake.

When lyrics appear in the song—as the Them guitarist Billy Harrison once put it so perfectly, when Morrison begins to "throw words at it"—you notice for the first time that there haven't been any. Suddenly what was chaos, unformed, threatening, thrilling, a giant, gaping mouth—is now a story. There's a singer and he's going to tell you about something, something about walking down by the old graveyard and looking into the eyes of the dead. But then that breaks up, too. "Eyes," he says again and again, the word fraying with each repetition, slipping the "mystic" that stands at its head, except when it doesn't. Morrison seems to turn away from the word, from words altogether, as if only fools actually believe that phonemes can signify, that a word is what it names, that there's any chance of understanding anything at all. The moment doesn't have the force, the desire—the termite instinct, as the critic Manny Farber unearthed it, of "doing go-for-broke art and not caring what comes of it"—of the first rampage of the music, which is like the harshest instrumental passage of Howlin' Wolf's 1951 "How Many More Years" turning into its own monster and turning against its own song. But the moment has its own humanity, which everywhere else is abstract: that half-second when the particular person singing the song's words gives up on words, in frustration, in disgust, in triumph, fully entering the music as himself and nobody else, throwing a single "eyes" against the wall with the knowledge that neither it nor any other words will ever catch a half of what he means. You're caught up in an irresolvable adventure that is taking place as you listen, in the notion that you can drop someone into the middle of a story and then jerk him or her out of it as if it were nothing more than a few minutes on the radio, now a bad dream you're certain is yours alone.

Them, "Mystic Eyes" (Parrot, US, Decca, UK, 1965). Included on *Them* (Parrot, 1965) and *The Angry Young Them* (Decca, 1965). Collected on *The Story of Them Featuring Van Morrison* (Polydor, 1998).

TUPELO HONEY, 1971

Florida Tupelo Honey is one of the rarest honeys with an exquisite buttery flavor and light color. Tupelo trees thrive along the rivers and creeks of the Florida panhandle and have delicate fragrant blossoms that can produce wonderful tupelo honey crops.

The Florida Tupelo flower is very delicate and blooms for only a very short time every year. Our beekeepers go through great lengths to keep our Florida tupelo honey pure by taking all the honey boxes off the hives and putting on clean empty beeswax combs right as the first tupelo flowers bloom. After about two weeks of bloom, we go out and take the honey boxes off the hives and spin it out to get the rare tupelo honey.

The Tupelo blossoms have very delicate little pistols that secrete the nectar. A strong wind or hard rain can rip the blossoms from the trees.

The blossoming period generally starts about the 20th of April every year and lasts about 3 weeks.

The honeybees are very eager to visit the blossoms, as the nectar can be quite abundant in good years.

Tupelo trees thrive in the river and creek bottoms where it is very wet.

—Sleeping Bear Farms, Beulah, Mississippi, 2009

Tupelo Honey was Van Morrison's gorgeous Woodstock album. It featured tinted photos of Morrison, his wife, and horses, including one of Morrison dressed like a country squire, all woodsy splendor. At the time, the record was like propaganda for the notion of leaving the strife of the previous decade behind and starting a new life, free of care. One of the songs was even called "Starting a New Life." There was "Old, Old Woodstock," "When That Evening Sun Goes Down," "You're My Woman," "I Wanna Roo You" ("Scottish Derivative," read the parenthetical subtitle, not that you needed a translation), "Moonshine Whiskey." Like "Wild Night," the single that leaped onto the radio in a flash and lost its luster almost as quickly, constant airplay making its celebration of kids out on the street feel tinsel cheap, a record anybody could have made and hundreds of people already had, the songs were cartoons. Today they make me think of the "War Free Edition" of the *New York Times* people buy in Jonathan Lethem's novel *Chronic City.* They make me think even more of something Dominique Robertson, then Robbie Robertson's wife, said to me when not long after *Tupelo Honey* appeared I went to Woodstock to talk to Robertson about the Band. I was seduced by the bucolic ease of this little corner of upstate New York, a world apart, but she wasn't. "Look at all this," she said, her hand waving toward the window opening onto the mountains, the forests, the sun. "It's everything people ought to want, and I hate it." "'This country life is killin' me,'" she sang, making up a song likely no one else in town would have thought of in that moment in history. "There's nothing here but dope, music, and beauty. If you're a woman, and you don't make music and you don't use dope, there's nothing here at all."

Maybe you could have heard that leaking through the cracks of Morrison's songs; a place where even the chirping of the birds seemed to bless your love was too good to be true. But the most gorgeous number on the album was the title song, and it was too good not to be true.

At almost seven unfolding minutes, it was a kind of odyssey. The constant invocation of "Tupelo honey" couldn't not invoke Elvis Presley; he too was smiling over the song's golden couple, as if they were living out all the best hopes of "Can't Help Falling in Love." It began with the most reassuring organ sound, gently picked notes on a guitar, a vocal that caressed the first verse, then ached through the chorus. You could miss the scrambled imagery of freed slaves and Camelot, "the road to freedom" and "knights in armor bent on chivalry"; you could catch it and feel part of a drama whose beginnings were lost in time and that would never end. "She's an angel," Morrison sang. "She's an angel," repeated the male voices behind him, the big, friendly sound of men who are jealous only of the fact that they're not as deserving as the singer has proven himself to be.

Morrison's voice grew bigger as the song went on, his singing more expansive, words turning into gestures, his arms spread wide, a finger pointing to the sky. "Yes she is," he almost whispered back at the chorus, as if answering himself in his own mind. "Yes she is!" he'd say elsewhere, banishing all doubt. The music went forward in steady steps, the knights sure in their mission, King Arthur with Excalibur in his hands.

The song had opened with an odd four lines, an old saying that seemed to come out of nowhere and go back there. "You can take. All the tea in China. Put it in a big brown bag for me. Sail right round all the seven oceans. Drop it straight into the deep blue sea." As Morrison smoothed the words, they struck a balance that gave the song as it moved on both its lightness and its weight—but finally there comes a point when all of this comes to a halt. Morrison has been all but kissing his words, lolling over them; then his clearwater tone breaks, and he takes a breath. The band drops back. "You can take," Morrison says, "all the tea in Chiney"—and with "Chiney," the vulgar word capsizing the ship, the scene shifts from the Woodstock hills and the open seas of the seven oceans to a Belfast wharf where an ugly old man is trying to sell you something you know you shouldn't want, and someone else over there in the shadows is waiting for a chance to expose himself. "Drop it, smack dab, in the middle of the deep blue sea," Morrison says, with the "smack dab" hit hard, the first word percussive, like a slap in the face, the "Drop it" instantly producing the image not of a bag of tea but of a gun, the singer daring anyone to stop him, to question him, and a smell of violence rises to the surface of the line.

"*Because*—" he announces: because she's as sweet as Tupelo honey, even if, for a second, the face that gets slapped by smack is hers. Literally, the words say that it doesn't matter what the world is or what it throws at me: love conquers all.

But as music, as words changing as they're spoken, they say nothing clearly. "All the tea in Chiney," then that "*Because*—" those words as they jump out of the song and bang up against each other make as true a yarragh, a breach, as any other. They can mean "Top of the world"—with James Cagney's murderous, self-immolating "Ma!" right on top of that. They can be funny. They can be crafty, inveigling, secretive, illegal. They can say, as the song says elsewhere, "You can't stop us." They can say *fuck it*. But whatever they say, that so strangely confiding "Chiney," a single word carrying a whole world of old movies up its sleeve, Charlie Chan prowling an opium den, Marlene Dietrich telling you "It took more than one man to change my name to Shanghai Lily," the peremptory, dismissively final "Drop it, smack dab, in the middle," they all take what appeared to be the song away from itself. In the middle of "Tupelo Honey" you can feel the rumble of "Mystic Eyes."

The first time I heard the song, this passage was like a bump in the road, and I drove right over it. Ever since, it's been the whole song, the part of the story that I wait for, like a punch line that no matter how many times you've heard it before never loses its sting.

Jonathan Lethem, *Chronic City* (New York: Doubleday, 2009).
Van Morrison, "Tupelo Honey," on *Tupelo Honey* (Warner Bros., 1971).

BABY PLEASE DON'T GO. 1965

In 1965, Them's "Baby Please Don't Go"—usually cited as a rock 'n' roll update of a song first recorded by the Mississippi blues singer Joe Williams—had the virtue of sounding as if it had emerged full-blown from Van Morrison's forehead. After a twenty-five-second lead-in—knife-edge notes on a guitar, following footsteps from a bass, drums and organ kicking up noise, harmonica curving the rhythm—Morrison leaps into the song as if he hasn't noticed the musical horde racing ahead, and as with "Mystic Eyes" in an instant the band is chasing him. There's a desperation in his hurry that all but rewrites the song: he's singing "Well, your man done gone," but you can hear it as "Your mind done gone" and believe it.

"It's so frantic," said my friend Phil Marsh, a guitarist in Berkeley in 1965, at a time when the country blues—the likes of Joe Williams' Washboard Blues Singers' 1935 original, a rickety, windblown number with fiddle and washboard that was like a shack, or Williams's 1940 remake with John Lee Williamson, the first Sonny Boy, on harmonica, which was like a fishing skiff on a lake, rocking every time a man cast but still when he waited—was a religion: a religion of fatalism, in which there was no hurry. But Them's "Baby Please Don't Go" isn't frantic. Just as you don't see Morrison coming, you're not ready when the music empties out. The band, at first onto the song like a flare shot in the air, begins to fragment. As the bassist pushes against the beat, poking it, the guitarist, the session player Jimmy Page or not, seems to be feeling his way into another song, flipping half-riffs, high, random, distracted metal shavings. Though the excitement of the music doesn't flag for a second, silence—anticipation— seems in command. Something is going to happen. You don't know what.

All sorts of people had recorded "Baby Please Don't Go," or the song inside it, "Alabama Bound," before Them seized it.* Lead Belly's 1940 "Alabama Bound," with the Golden Gate Jubilee Quartet, could be a bunch of guys with their arms around each other exiting a bar. ("I'm going back tomorrow," one man says. "Me, too, boy," says another.) Lightnin' Hopkins's glowing 1948 recording of "Baby Please Don't

---

* And after: Morrison recorded "Alabamy Bound" with Lonnie Donegan and Chris Barber as part of *The Skiffle Sessions*, the album recorded at Whitla Hall in Belfast in 1998. Donegan starts slowly, not hiding his English accent, Barber hiding his even less so when he takes the song, but when Morrison comes in, first singing background, then swallowing the song whole, he sounds like a sea monster, and his accent seems to have been something the song was searching for all along.

Go," with the Texas singer accompanying himself on electric guitar, was full, open, and endlessly suggestive of what Hopkins was deliberately leaving out of the piece, for the wind that whistled around the notes he hung in the air.

Morrison would have known these records; so likely would Jimmy Page, or, assuming Morrison was borrowing his father's 78s or bringing his friends around, even Them guitarist Billy Harrison.

What did it mean for young people to discover the old country blues in the early 1960s? For some, like Phil Marsh, it meant the reverence due a religion, and they played the old songs to capture their notes, their melodies, their flourishes, as precisely as possible, as if to pass down the truth unadulterated and uncorrupted. But others heard the radicalism of the country blues: the ferocity, the way in which within the structures of an all but unalterable musical form there were no limits at all to the demands one might make on himself or herself, on those around them, on life as such. Others were drawn to the statements of black men and women who if they acted in everyday life as they acted in their songs would have had groundhogs delivering their mail. What they wanted to capture was the spirit of singers who somehow summoned the nerve to sing about the world as if it remained to be made, or as if it could be unmade. Thus Van Morrison's "Baby Please Don't Go" is harsh, the whole performance slashing through paper walls.

Quickly, there's nothing between the singer and the song: no reverence, no respect, no hesitation in taking the fruits of someone else's culture. If one's own response to that culture—the culture as set down by a small number of people in Mississippi and elsewhere in the American South from the late 1920s to the early '40s—is as strong as Van Morrison's plainly was, how can that culture not be in the deepest sense one's own? One learns the language in order to speak the song—in order to speak out loud in the world. In 1965, Them's "Baby Please Don't Go" was out loud, on the radio, and its yarragh was its heedlessness.

Joe Williams' Washboard Blues Singers, "Baby Please Don't Go" (Williams, guitar; Dad Tracy, one-string fiddle; Chasey Collins, washboard, Chicago, 1935, Bluebird), collected on *Harry Smith's Anthology of American Folk Music, Volume Four* (Revenant, 2000).

Joe Williams, "Please Don't Go" (Williams, guitar; John Lee "Sonny Boy" Williams, harmonica; Alfred Elkins, bass cano, Chicago, 1941, Bluebird), included on *The Roots of Van Morrison* (Complete Blues, 2008).

Lead Belly and the Golden Gate Jubilee Quartet (Willie Johnson, William Langford, Henry Owens, Arlandus Wilson, Chicago, 1940, Victor), "Alabama Bound," on Lead Belly, *Alabama Bound* (RCA, 1988).

Lightnin' Hopkins, "Baby Please Don't Go" (Houston, 1948, 1949, Gold Star), on *Mojo Hand: Lightnin' Hopkins Anthology* (Rhino, 1993).

Them, "Baby Please Don't Go" (Parrot, US, Decca, UK, 1965). Collected on *The Story of Them Featuring Van Morrison* (Polydor, 1998). Flipside of "Gloria," the band's second single.

Van Morrison with Lonnie Donegan and Chris Barber, "Alabamy Bound," *The Skiffle Sessions* (Virgin, 2000).

JOHN BROWN'S BODY. 1975

The sense of a search is alive in this fugitive recording, even if the recording itself never comes to life. Sometimes Morrison's failures stick faster than the successes of countless other honorable singers.

It's a rehearsal, or a warm-up for what the people present are actually there to do. Someone snaps strings on an old guitar. Someone else plays the kind of war-movie harmonica notes that the comedian Robert Klein describes as being played in every Civil War picture, "around the campfire," before the next massacre: "Boy?" "Yes, sir?" "Ever been in a battle before?" "No, sir—but I'm aimin' to." "Better stop playin' that goddamn harmonica!" A piano keeps time.

"John Brown body lie molding in a grave," Morrison begins, as if not quite remembering the words, and in a voice so creaky you're not immediately sure it's his. The piece comes through as a lost song, an air that hasn't been sung

27

for generations, that's survived in the common imagination only in bare fragments: "Glory, glory, hallelujah, his truth go marching on." Morrison tries to pump it as a drummer bashes cymbals—"Yeah! Mmm-hmm. I like it. Oh! Look out! Brand new thang!"—but the exclamations sound like vocal exercises.

Then the song sucks him back. He's singing as someone panning for gold, finding nothing but sand, running his hands through the water. He crouches there, waiting for the song to give itself up, to surrender its secrets. But an unidentified violinist—probably not Toni Marcus, the violinist who will appear with Morrison on his *Into the Music* four years later, but I like to think so, so I'll pretend it's her—has been there all along, following Morrison's slow footsteps, looking for a theme—and finally, you might hear, she's had enough. This song is not a secret to her, and she begins to sing it, on her strings, with more blood, loss, and an embrace of a right cause than Morrison can, or will. It's all in the high notes, with an urgency that says she's hearing hidden strains in the song no one has heard before—but as she begins to light up the sky the song as it was composed always reached for, the sky comes down to earth, and for a last moment Morrison steps up to claim the song as if he knew it all along.

Robert Klein, "In Praise of the Harmonica," on *Mind Over Matter* (Rhino, 1974).

Van Morrison, "John Brown's Body," collected on *Catalog Strays 1965–2000* (Wild Card bootleg).

CARAVAN. *THE LAST WALTZ.* 1976

"If he had much stage presence it'd be hard to take," a friend said after seeing Van Morrison perform this song, not long after its release on *Moondance*, in 1970, Morrison's first album after *Astral Weeks*. He'd stand still on stage to sing it, needing only "Now the caravan, is on its way," the first line, to bring him into the setting of the song—a hillside in the country, you could imagine, a line of wood-covered vans or trailers, filled with gypsies or their would-be middle-class inheritors, whoever it might have been with the destiny or the choice to live on the road getting a moment in history through the way the song pushed out of it. You might feel the Impressions' "Gypsy Woman" behind Morrison's song—a long way behind it, dubious, Curtis Mayfield wondering if any song that mentioned gypsies could really summon up the campfires that in his song really did seem to flicker in the listener's eye. Morrison would point his head down with his eyes closed, as if he were trying to answer Mayfield's doubt. "Turn up your radio," he'd whisper the first time the line appeared in the song; the second time it would be a plea, desperate and enthralled, and now there was an answer. It was on the radio. You just had to turn it up, so you didn't miss it. It's easy to miss something on the radio; you turn your head, say "Did you hear that" or "Listen to this," and it's gone, and the DJ isn't going to understand when you call to ask what it was whoever the singer was did right before the instrumental break. "Turn it up"—but not too much, not so the curls in the singer's voice on the radio are flattened with volume and the soul is gone: "That's enough!" Morrison would always shout, just when the perfect level was reached, like someone who has to be touched just this way. Do it right, and it's heaven; squeeze a little too hard, move your hand an inch in the wrong direction, and love turns to ashes. All of that is happening in "Caravan," in the instant.

By the time Morrison recorded his first live album, " . . . *It's Too Late to Stop Now . . .* " from 1974, the song had become a rave-up, almost a set-closer—a crowd favorite—but that night it couldn't find its voice. Curtis Mayfield turned his head. The tempo was too fast—the oldest musician's trick in the oldest book to spark false excitement in a familiar number. Then it stopped, to insist on drama; you could see the levers and pulleys. The music is ornamented, filigreed, the song buried in so many layers of orchestration that the choruses, the heart of the song—"TURN IT UP! TURN IT UP!"—never did more than shout. Morrison took time to introduce the band, then seemed to drift off, murmuring "Now for the best, later for the garbage," as if talking to himself, and it might have been the most true and least forced moment in the performance.

Two years later, at the Last Waltz, the Band's Thanksgiving night farewell concert at Winterland in San Francisco, with the bill heavy with guest stars, the show, which produced a certain streak of tedium that lifted only for two or three numbers at a time, had come nearly to a halt. After a few mountain turns of a runaway train—the Band playing inside out for "Mystery Train" with Paul Butterfield, for "Who Do You Love" with their old mentor, the 1950s rockabilly flash Ronnie Hawkins, and then, titanically, almost seven minutes of "Mannish Boy" led by Muddy Waters— the show lost its breath. Waters was followed by Eric Clapton, Neil Young, Joni Mitchell, and Neil Diamond; the sense of I'll-never-forget-this-night the crowd had brought with them and the Band itself had insisted on (an unheard-of ticket price, a full Thanksgiving dinner, curtains from the opera house, chandeliers flown in from Los Angeles) began to disappear, replaced by mere stargazing. People in the audience began to speculate about who else might show up. One fan predicted that Buddy Holly would appear precisely at midnight. Another person claimed to have seen Murry Wilson—the then recently deceased father of three-fifths of the Beach Boys—backstage. Someone yelled out for "Free Bird."

Morrison was next—the last guest before the very last, Bob Dylan—and he turned the night around. "I always go by what gets the most house," said Dr. John, himself one of the first Last Waltz guests, flat on his own "Such a Night," a haunt on "Liza Jane" with the New Orleans singer Bobby Charles. "To me, Van Morrison got the most house, of anything. I was checkin' the gig," he said in his crawly voice, the gutter growl of a man who hasn't been impressed by anything since 1957, "and it was like, the whole gig, it got house. 'Cause mostly, you know, it's like famous people . . . But nuttin' was like that. Nuttin' got that much house. That was way above anything else. That was a hard act to follow."

At the rehearsal the night before, where Martin Scorsese, who was filming the concert, or rather directing it—with every song plotted, every shot blocked, lighting designed to vary what would appear on a screen—"Caravan" was already a showstopper, and there wasn't even a show. Morrison stepped right into it, the Band playing easily behind him, staying out of his way, Allen Toussaint's horn section working from arrangements that were fixed in meter but still had room in them. "Now the caravan is on its way," Morrison sang, not a word rushed, no melodramatic pause, simply the first line of an old story everybody knows. You say "Once upon a time," not "Once—upon a time," unless you're full of yourself, or you don't trust the audience. Morrison may not trust his audience, but this night there wasn't one.

At the show itself you could imagine that the song grew bigger than it ever had before. Again and again there is an increase in pressure, then release. You are constantly aware of the back of the throat. Nothing is abstract, nothing is taken for granted. "Turn up your radio": "radio" becomes "RAD-IO"—

RAADIO

—and suddenly it's not a radio, it's a Flash Gordon death ray. The horn section locks into a pattern, *dah* da da *dah*, drawn out more every time,

DAHHHH da da *DAH!*

Again and again, there's a freer theme to highlight the hard count, and as the horn section pushed back, louder each time, Morrison matching it in volume, he began to kick his right leg into the air like a Rockette. He shot an arm up, a dynamo, the movements repeated, repeated, repeated, and shocking every time. Finally as he left the stage he was swaying from side to side, his body all vehemence, his face in the placid, self-circled expression of someone who hears nothing but the song playing in his head. All in all it signified that finally he had taken everything the song had to give, he had left nothing out, making you stare and ask, where did this person come from, why is he here? It was always a song that demanded to be made a testimony—*this is the last song I'm ever going to sing in my life*—and that's what Morrison gave back. Edwyn Collins, the singer for the Glasgow band Orange Juice, once remembered his manager crying after a performance: "The big moments are never as good as you think they're going to be." This night they were—but before any of this happened there was a rupture that broke the ground for the performance, and it had nothing to do with music.

"At rehearsal, when we went over this," Robbie Robertson said in commentary for the video release of *The Last Waltz*, "he came in and he had just flown in from somewhere. I guess he'd come right from the airport, and he was wearing a raincoat, maybe it had been raining, I don't remember now, but he had on this Mickey Spillane–looking raincoat. And I thought, you know what? This detective thing, this Humphrey Bogart detective thing, is working for me. And I said to Van, 'I like this, I like this Mike Hammer thing you got going here—you should wear this outfit tonight.' And he said, 'You think so? You really like it?' 'It works. It's definitely working.' And he said, 'Oh, ok.' And that night, when it came time for the show, as you can see, he felt more the need to dress for the occasion."

As the dishes were being cleared from the Thanksgiving tables, I'd seen Morrison wandering the still mostly empty aisles in Winterland, dressed in his raincoat, scowling. He was thirty; he looked older, pudgy and losing his hair. It was surprising to see him appear onstage like a grimy Cinderella in a purple stage suit: a spangled bolero jacket, sausage pants with contrasting lacing up the crotch, a green top with a scoop neck that produced what could only be called cleavage. *God*, you thought—*where did he get this thing?* Who drugged him, knocked him out, dragged him into a costume store, and put this on him and said, *Well, here you are, you look* great, *Van, you look just terrific!* It was as if he was daring the audience, or for that matter the Band, not to see past the ludicrousness of his costume ("I remember a couple of times becoming completely distracted and felt like I was in the audience," Robertson said), not to see what he was doing, not to hear the music.

"Van always looked to me like a half-homicidal leprechaun who lived under the bridge," the critic Jay Cocks likes to say. For a night he came out from under the bridge. Then he went back. It was stunning; no one remarked on the slime dripping from his elbows, the bits of dead rats on his shoes.

Quotes from *The Last Waltz* (MGM DVD, 1978/2002).

Edwyn Collins, "This Much I Know," interview with Michael Odell (2008), in *Best Music Writing 2009*, ed. GM (New York: Da Capo, 2009), 287.

Impressions, "Gypsy Woman" (ABC-Paramount, 1961).

Van Morrison, "Caravan," *Moondance* (Warner Bros., 1970).

———"Caravan," on *". . . It's Too Late to Stop Now . . ."* (Warner Bros., 1974).

———"Caravan" (rehearsal and performance), included on the Band, *The Last Waltz* box set (Warner Bros./Rhino, 2002), and on DVD as above.

IT'S ALL OVER NOW, BABY BLUE. 1966

When Bob Dylan first began performing "It's All Over Now, Baby Blue," the song that would close his album *Bringing It All Back Home*, released in the spring of 1965, no one had heard it before. It would come at the end of a concert, and it would be a shock—not for its melody, or its words, or its tinge of finality (in the summer of that year, at the Newport Folk Festival, Dylan would sing it as his farewell to those in the crowd who had booed him for appearing with a band), but for what Dylan was doing with his arms.

He would bend over his guitar, thrust his arms out from it akimbo, and begin to flap them up and down, as if he were a puppet and the strings were his own rhythm, and the rhythm in the song was big, loose, dramatic, and unsatisfied. No matter how hard Dylan pumped, there was something missing, and that seemed to be the point. Performing

solo for the last season before he began, first with pickup
groups and then with the Arkansas-Canadian quintet the
Hawks, to present his songs as he was hearing them in his
head—hearing them, you can imagine, as the Beatles or the
Rolling Stones or the Animals might have done them, but
not as well, he had to know, as he would—what the performance dramatized was the absence of the power the song
itself wanted.

"It's All Over Now, Baby Blue" cried out for a band. At
the Avalon Ballroom in San Francisco in 1966, the Grateful
Dead were among the first to try, barely—Jerry Garcia's lead
guitar was still light with respect. It was still a folk song; for
that matter it was less rock 'n' roll than Dylan's own recording, with Bruce Langhorne's distant, milky electric guitar
notes shadowing the themes Dylan was stating on his own
strings.

What was missing, perhaps, was a sense that the song was
taking place in a world that was not quite the real world, and
that the person to whom the song was addressed was in danger; that was what the song said when Van Morrison recorded it with Them late in 1965. When it appeared in 1966
on the group's second album, *Them Again*, it was first of all
strange. As they listened to Them, people who already knew
the song by heart weren't certain they had ever heard it before. You can imagine Bob Dylan might have felt the same—
or at least as he might have when he first heard Sam Cooke
sing "Blowin' in the Wind." It's one thing to send a song out
into the world on the strength of a voice made of conviction;
it's another to have it come back to you as an eagle.

"The feeling that music can create in a listener doesn't come from our opinion or image of the artist who makes the music, if our response is at all genuine," Jon Landau wrote of the Doors and the Memphis soul duo Sam and Dave in 1968. "It doesn't come from the artist telling us what he's trying to do or acting it out. It is there in the way he says the words more than in what the words say. And if Jim Morrison screams at us to 'Break on through to the other side,' well, Sam and Dave don't have to tell us about it because their music is *on* the other side." That's where Them is with "It's All Over Now, Baby Blue."

It begins like the first page of a detective novel, with three clipped, odd bass patterns, like a knock on the door, but with an odd fatalism: the cadence says that the person knocking is going in whether anyone opens the door or not, or that he already knows what he's going to find. "I knocked two longs and two shorts as instructed," the notes say, as Raymond Chandler says in *The Little Sister*. "Nothing happened. I felt jaded and old. I felt as if I'd spent my life knocking at doors in cheap hotels that nobody bothered to open. I tried again. Then turned the knob and walked in," but this time when Philip Marlowe walks in he finds that behind the door of Room 332 in the Van Nuys Hotel is a black hole.

It's a scene set by dark and shapeless notes from an electric piano; they sweep you off your feet. As Morrison comes in, singing deliberately, there are sharp, bright notes from an acoustic guitar, a deepening of the piano sound from an electric guitar, what could be a single chord from an organ sustained for the whole performance, but what's uncanny is

that while the emotional pressure of the performance continues to rise, Morrison bearing down harder verse by verse,
the overwhelming sense of displacement, of being in the
wrong place at the wrong time, comes entirely from the
piano, and the way that throughout the performance it remains altogether on the same plane. It's this that creates an
atmosphere of unrelieved suspense and jeopardy.

You're catching no more than a glimpse of an ongoing
drama. The detective walks right in, but then he vanishes,
and the people in the room—the person speaking, the person he or she is speaking to—are not leaving, and not because, as with the person Marlowe finds—

Beyond the little hallway the room widened towards a pair of windows through which the evening sun slanted in a shaft that reached
almost across the bed and came to a stop under the neck of the man
that lay there. What it stopped on was blue and white and shining
and round. He lay quite comfortably half on his face with his hands
down at his sides and his shoes off. The side of his face was on the
pillow and he seemed relaxed. He was wearing a toupee. The last time
I had talked to him his name had been George W. Hicks. Now it was
Dr. G. W. Hambleton. Same initials. Not that it mattered anymore. I
wasn't going to be talking to him again. There was no blood. None at
all, which is one of the nice things about an expert ice-pick job

—they're dead. They're in a limbo Dylan's recording hardly
hints at, which is why in his performance "Drawing crazy
patterns on your sheets" is unsurprising and why when
Morrison sings the line it's frightening.

It wasn't a story for the asking. Invited on stage for an encore at a Bob Dylan show at Wembley Arena in London in 1984, Morrison took up the song once more. "After it's written, I release the words"—that can be true for anything Morrison sings. It doesn't matter whose words they are. But with Dylan's band locked into a hand-clapping beat, a wail that lifted "crying" out of "Crying like an orphan in the sun" only gave the word an instant's flight. Even against Chrissie Hynde's high, keening shouts on the title phrase at the end of every verse the singalong crowd's insistence that the song not only couldn't but shouldn't speak anything other than a dead language ruled.

Jon Landau, "Soul Men," *Rolling Stone*, 20 January 1968, 18.

Raymond Chandler, *The Little Sister* (1949; New York: Pocket Books, 1963), 36, 38.

Bob Dylan, "It's All Over Now, Baby Blue," on *Bringing It All Back Home* (Columbia, 1965).

Them, "It's All Over Now, Baby Blue," on *Them Again* (Parrot, US, Decca, UK, 1966), included on *The Story of Them Featuring Van Morrison* (Polydor, 1998).

Van Morrison, "It's All Over Now, Baby Blue," London, 7 July 1984, on *Whenever Bob Sheds His Light on Van* (bootleg).

PART TWO

I'M GOING TO MY GRAVE WITH THIS RECORD

ASTRAL WEEKS. 1968

From the sightlines in Berkeley, California, where I lived then and live now, I recall 1968 as a year of horror and bad faith, fervor and despair. Most of all there was the sense of knowing that when you drew a breath you were breathing history along with the air, or the smoke—but that doesn't mean you knew what history was, or would be. History was being made in the instant, which said nothing about what would be included in the books yet to be written, or left out of them, as if what goes in and what goes out stays the same. These names made history in 1968: John Carlos, Bob Beamon, Tommie Smith. They were shouted around the world. Which still echo, which is barely a name at all? "Still the spirit of '68," John Lydon, born to the world as Johnny Rotten, sang in 1979 with his band PiL, when 1968, not a concept but a year, a real time, seemed much farther away than, in this era of media anniversaries, it does now. The song was "Albatross"; the singer sounded beaten down by history, 1968 a huge bird around his neck, but he also sounded as if he knew the beating wings were the wind at his back.

Berkeley was a lookout and a hideout. The great storm of student protest that would convulse the U.S.A. and nations around the world had begun there in 1964 with the Free Speech Movement. It was three months of daily speeches, marches, building occupations, and finally, played out in a Greek Theatre, high drama. That drama—a university in convocation with itself, everyone present, the leaders of the institution speaking quieting words, then a single student, standing to speak, immediately tackled and dragged out of sight, an act of violence actually revealing the face of power behind the face of reasonableness—brought that moment to a close and opened a field that in the years to come would be crossed by thousands. But in 1968 the spirit that animated a simple demand for the free exercise of rights students had assumed were theirs—because they had learned such a story in their classrooms and then, as if by instinct, began to put them into practice—had in the most familiar arena long since turned cheap and rote.

When in May of 1968 a rally was held in Berkeley to celebrate the poorly understood but exciting revolt taking place in France, activists distributed leaflets denouncing the police violence that had dispersed the rally before the rally took place. When students at Columbia University in New York, protesting what they saw as the university's colonialist appropriation of property in Harlem, shut the school down—

with the novel technique of occupying one building, and then, when the police arrived, filing out, only to seize another building, and then another, and another—Berkeley radicals called on their fellows to "Do a Columbia": not for any reason, not in the face of any injustice or insult, but for lack of anything better to do.

With the Vietnam War all but rolling back across the Pacific to poison the United States itself, it was as if people turned to spectacular lies and glamorous trivialities to hide from themselves the fact that their imaginations had turned to ice. Truly enormous events taking place elsewhere did not travel. Word of Prague Spring, even the meaning of the Soviet invasion that crushed it, arrived only in fragments, and no speaker stood up to put the pieces together. News of the massacre of hundreds of students in Mexico City, just before the Olympic Games were to begin there, was suppressed from the start, and so profoundly that the facts would take nearly forty years to come out of the ground. But in the United States few if any looked; curiosity about the world withered.

It's clear now that the signal song of that year, the song with which all through the 1990s and into the twenty-first century Bob Dylan closed his concerts, was "All Along the Watchtower"—a modest, querulous song that ended with words that were anything but quiet, regardless of how simply they were sung: "Two riders were approaching / The wind began to howl." The song occupied the moral center of Dylan's album *John Wesley Harding*, which was released in the last week of 1967; like the rest of the music, those words of warning made their way onto and out of the radio slowly, like a rumor. Too slowly: when Martin Luther King, Jr., was assassinated in Memphis in April, and then, in June, in Los Angeles, Robert F. Kennedy, running for president, was shot and killed, the song did not play, even in the minds of those who watched the funerals on television. It did not give voice to the awful sense of disease, ruin, and damnation that seized the country so fully it could only be channeled into pathetic calls for gun control and a ludicrous riot in Chicago against a presidential nominating convention where, had he lived, Kennedy would have almost certainly lost. To play against these events, to play into them, the song needed the harsher, louder, wilder, even triumphant treatment Neil Young would give it in 1992—an arrangement Dylan himself immediately adopted—and that Van Morrison could have fashioned at any time.

The Mexican government wanted a clean Olympics, a clean show, and so did the world. That is why the massacres took place, why the government buried the event literally and figuratively, and why the cover-up was a complete success, with witnesses disappeared or conventionally murdered for years afterward to keep the peace. So the games went on as planned—except for John Carlos and Tommie Smith of San Jose State in California, American entrants in the two hundred–meter dash. Inspired by Harry Edwards's Olympic Project for Human Rights, which had originally called for a boycott of the Olympics by all black athletes, they had a plan. They would run the race; they would win; they would mount the victory stand; and then, as the band played "The

Star-Spangled Banner," before the eyes of the entire world they would bow their heads and raise black-gloved fists in salutes of black power and black unity. With beads around their necks they would signify the deaths of those leaders like King who had been assassinated, and the nameless thousands gone who had been lynched and thrown from slave ships; with shoeless feet they would signify poverty; in their silence they would speak out. On October 16 the plan was realized: Smith finished first, tying the world record, and took the gold medal, Carlos finished third and took the bronze. As Peter Norman of Australia, who took the silver medal—and who, that night, would wear an Olympics Project for Human Rights badge in solidarity—stared straight ahead, Smith and Carlos gestured.

They marked, or scarred, their national anthem as definitively as Jimi Hendrix would a year later at Woodstock. Though no one, as far as I know, drew the connection at the time, Hendrix's furiously, exultantly distorted, bottomlessly complex recasting of "The Star-Spangled Banner" was not only a version of what Smith and Carlos did with it, his version may have been inspired by theirs.

This event has never been forgotten. Carlos and Smith were treated as terrorists, as if their fists were guns and they had fired them. They were expelled from their team, sent home, and covered in obloquy. Though they never backed down, as the years passed neither man's affirmation of what he had done matched the other's. There were disagreements over whose idea the act was, over who owned it. As they do still, across the decades interviewers worked to draw out

48	GREIL MARCUS

resentment and betrayal, to find a crack in the image of the two men on the stand that for all of the confusion added to it after the fact remains indelibly plain.

On October 18, two days after Smith and Carlos were removed from the games, the American long-jumper Bob Beamon launched himself. He had never jumped farther than twenty-seven feet and four inches; he would never again jump farther than twenty-six feet and eleven and three-quarter inches. But this day, when he landed, he had become the first person in history to jump twenty-eight feet; he had become the first person in history to jump twenty-nine feet. He had traveled twenty-nine feet and two and one-half inches through the air. From 1935 to 1968 the world record in the long jump had increased by eight and a half inches; this day Bob Beamon broke the world record by almost two feet. When he saw his mark on the scoreboard, he fell to his knees and covered his face in shock.

It was an act for which there are no parallels and no metaphors. There can be no statue for it, as, in 2005, at San Jose State University, a statue was unveiled celebrating the act performed in 1968 by John Carlos and Tommie Smith: figures of the two men on the victory stand, with Peter Norman's place empty, so that, as Norman said when the statue was unveiled, "Anybody can get up there and stand up for something they believe in." "We felt a need to represent a lot of people who did more than we did and had no platform," Smith said. It was about human rights, Norman said: "The issue is still there today and they'll be there at Beijing and we've got to make sure we don't lose sight of that."*

Bob Beamon's name is little mentioned today. For twenty-three years, jumpers edged closer to his record, inch by inch; mathematically, it was finally broken by Michael Powell in 1991, but in the way that his act has never been matched, even in imagination it was never really surpassed. In 1968, almost everything became part of history even before people realized what had happened, and for the rest of their lives, they and

---

* Andrew Das, "Obama Fever on the Field," *New York Times*, 8 November 2008: "On Thursday night . . . after scoring the winning touchdown against the Browns with 1 minute and 22 seconds to go, [Denver Broncos receiver Brandon] Marshall reached into his pants and pulled out a glove before his teammates quickly surrounded him.

"Marshall told the NFL Network postgame crew: 'When we look at the 44th president, Barack Obama, he inspired me. And not just me and my teammates, but the nation.'

"Marshall said his planned celebration—which was stopped by teammate Brandon Stokely, who worried that a 15-yard penalty could cost the Broncos in a see-saw game—had its roots in the black power salutes of John Carlos and Tommie Smith at the 1968 Olympics.

"Carlos and Smith each wore a black glove for their salutes, but Marshall said his was black and white.

"'I wanted to create that symbol of unity because Obama inspires me, our multicultural society,' he told reporters after the game, stopping several times during his news conference as emotion overwhelmed him. 'And I knew at the 1968 Olympics in Mexico, Tommie Smith and John Carlos raised the black glove in that fist as a silent gesture of black power and liberation. Forty years later, I wanted to make my own statement and gesture to represent the progress we made.'

"Marshall probably would have been fined if he had carried out his salute, but he said, 'Social landmarks are bigger than fines to me, especially two days after the election.'"

others, many not born at the time, would argue over what
they had done. But what Bob Beamon did was in a queer and
ineradicable way outside of history, where it remains—and in
that sense, in a way different from all the banners raised
in 1968, it is an image of freedom against which there can be
no argument at all.

As I hear it now, and as I think I heard it then, *Astral
Weeks*, recorded in three days in September and October
1968 in New York City, and released on the Warner Bros.–
Seven Arts label in November, caught the same spirit. In
historical terms it didn't make sense. It didn't, in the small-
minded way art and politics are so often linked, reflect the
great events of the day, any more than Dylan's *John Wesley
Harding*, *Astral Weeks*' true kin, did. *John Wesley Harding*
might have been a testament that, as Jon Landau put it in
1968, "Dylan has felt the war," but in its quiet, its lack of
hurry, its insistence on setting its own pace, its refusal even
to acknowledge that the person whose name was on the album cover had ever done anything before, it like *Astral
Weeks* refused to speak the language of the time, and in the
way that the time has been rewritten into a single rotting
cliché of VIETNAM STUDENT RIOTS LBJ LSD SEXUAL
REVOLUTION BLACK POWER NIXON neither *John Wesley Harding* nor *Astral Weeks* can be translated back into
that language. "It did come out at a time when a lot of
things a lot of people cared about passionately were beginning to disintegrate, and when the self-destructive under-
tow that always accompanied the great sixties party had
an awful lot of ankles in its maw and was pulling straight

down," Lester Bangs wrote in 1978 about *Astral Weeks*. "So, as timeless as it finally is, perhaps *Astral Weeks* was also the product of an era." But it wasn't any yearning for the strife and revelations of another time that accounted for the fact that a few years ago, in a class I was teaching, four students out of sixteen, none of them older than twenty-one, named it as the album they most loved. How did it reach these people, just in the sense of from here to there, of round-about? How did it enter their lives, music that was made well before they were born and yet spoke a common language? The record spoke to these people then; as far as they cared it was made for them, they understood its language as soon as they heard it. No one had to translate it for them, no one had to contextualize it, no one had to offer them any lectures about the music or the politics of the late sixties or the career of Van Morrison.

If *Astral Weeks* caught the spirit of Bob Beamon's event, then it also partook of it. As I understand history, Bob Beamon's jump would not have happened as it did if the skies had been different that day in Mexico City, if he had received a call from his wife that morning, or a different call than he did, or if that day's paper that morning had carried a different story, and the same must have been true when the producer Lewis Merenstein brought Van Morrison into a studio with a few New York City jazzmen: the bassist Richard Davis, the drummer Connie Kay, the guitarist Jay Berliner, the percussionist and vibraphonist Warren Smith, Jr., and the flautist and soprano saxophonist John Payne. The music that resulted wasn't jazz. It wasn't blues. It wasn't rock 'n' roll in any ordinary or hyphenated manner, but it fit perfectly on the radio in between Jimi Hendrix's "Little Wing" or Otis Redding's "Try a Little Tenderness." It was closer to folk music, and closer to "Barbara Allen" or the Irish ballad "Raglan Road" than "We Shall Overcome" or even "Goodnight Irene."

Merenstein had received a call from Warner Bros.: *We've signed Van Morrison, go up to Boston, see what he's got.* Pretty much all anybody knew, and all anybody wanted, was "Brown-Eyed Girl," from *Blowin' Your Mind!* which my friend Barry Franklin described at the time as "two minutes and twenty-six seconds of 'Sweet Pea' and thirty-two minutes of 'T. B. Sheets.'" ("Is the B. in 'T. B. Sheets,'" he asked, "the same B. which appeared in 'Johnny B. Goode'?") Morrison played Merenstein his song "Astral Weeks": "thirty seconds into it," Merenstein told Hank Shteamer in 2009, "my whole being was vibrating." And the moment could not have been any different, Merenstein said, not the call going to Tom Wilson, the producer of "Like a Rolling Stone," who was standing nearby when the phone rang, not Connie Kay catching Napoleon's cold: "Something as timeless as forty years had to happen because it had to happen. I had to be the one to do it. Not that producer, not that producer, regardless of their accomplishments. It had to be Richard, not that bass player. I don't want to sound existential, but there was Van, and that was it; there was no band . . . there were no arrangements . . . the direction was him singing and playing—that was where I followed. That's why it came out the way it did. If I would've gone somewhere else, it wouldn't have come out the way it did. So there obviously was a direction from somewhere in the sky." "This is not an exaggeration, this is not just trying to be poetic," Brooks Arthur, the recording engineer for *Astral Weeks*, said in 2009. "A cloud came along, and it was called the Van Morrison sessions. We all hopped upon that cloud, and the cloud took us away for a while, and we made this album, and we landed when it was done."

They recorded live, Morrison saying nothing to the musicians in terms of banter or instruction, and saying everything in the cues of his chords, hesitations, lunges, silences, and in those moments when he loosed himself from words and floated on his own air. But that's too simple. When you listen, you hear the musicians talking to each other; more than that, you hear them hearing each other.

In the first notes of "Sweet Thing," Morrison opens the tune with his acoustic guitar; as soon as a listener has something to grab onto, Richard Davis restates Morrison's theme, with the barest increase in force that makes all the difference. Davis was born in Chicago; he was a veteran of sessions with Eric Dolphy and Roland Kirk. This day it's as if Davis is sweeping into the song to dance Morrison even farther into it—into *Astral Weeks'* great swirl. Someone other than Morrison is now leading the listener into the bower of the song, a hillside where you can tumble down like Jim and little Sabine in *Jules and Jim*; that gives Morrison the freedom to forget the shape of the song, what it needs, what it wants, and trust himself. He'll sing the song; someone else will play it.

After the sessions were finished, Merenstein, with Morrison and the conductor Larry Fallon consulting, overdubbed strings and horn parts. Sometimes the songs are unimaginable without them, and the added sounds so layered into the original instruments as to be part of them, as on "Sweet Thing"; sometimes they're gratuitous, especially the strings on "Cyprus Avenue" and the gypsy violin on "Madame George," but after forty years they tune themselves out. When the music is at its most contingent—when Merenstein's argument about how the record might never have happened at all becomes an awareness that the fate of a song, whether or not it will achieve the finality you in fact know it will, rests on the way Richard Davis steps out of a rest and whether or not Morrison will know what Davis has just done and what he himself can now do to live up to it— it's scary, because the inevitability of the music is also its unlikeliness. Early on, there's a rupture in "Sweet Thing" when Morrison hollers—a long, happy *hoyyyyyyyy*, the singer shot out of the cannon of his own breath—and the scene the sound makes is so complete, the musicians around Morrison filling in the "gardens all wet with rain" he's already described, that you realize no one has to go back to the song at all. Near the end of "Madame George"—almost two minutes from its actual end, but at the end of the song as a written piece, a story told in lines and verses, one after the other—there's a pause, and then, at seven minutes thirty-four seconds, a single thick, weighted bass note from Davis that is as final a sound as any song could hold without dropping dead on the spot. The story is over, the note says; everything that is going to happen has happened; everyone has been left behind; everyone is dead, and all that remains is looking back. Morrison goes on, drawing a seemingly endless loop of loss, regret, reverie, and escape around himself— as he does so, you are actually hearing him change from a child into a creature who may not yet be a man but who is not a child, who may no longer even be human, rather a figment of his own false memories—but Davis is finished. Every note he plays after that last one is sweeping up, closing the windows, locking the door. At this point the song is as much his as Morrison's; both have their own ideas about what it's for, what it's about, who Madame George is, and why anyone should care: why in their different ways they are going to make you care. At its highest pitch, the album has become a collaboration between Morrison and Davis, or a kind of conspiracy, one that takes advantage of the producer and the other musicians but excludes them from the real conversation—excludes them, but somehow not the listener. In the blues term for the shadow self that knows what the self refuses to know, here Davis is Morrison's second mind; there Morrison is Davis's. You are listening in, but you can never be sure you heard what you thought you heard.

There is death all over the music—an acceptance of death. Save for one couplet, the last words on the album are a farewell, in the form of a closing door: "I know you're dying— and I know, you know it too." Davis rattles the door in its frame. But usually death is not so close. It's something you see in someone's face, maybe years off, but already looming. You freeze up—or you realize you have no time to waste. You begin asking what it is you really want. In the title song the singer asks to be born again—"There you go," he says to himself in the mirror, or to the person who he expects will save him, "talking to Hudie Ledbetter." Lead Belly died in 1949, almost twenty years before, only four years after the person singing was born, but he's here now, and he'll answer you if you know how to ask. And for a moment you do. "Would you, kiss my eyes"—what a surrender of body and soul are in those lines! It's an opening into what Lester Bangs called the "mystical awe that cut right through the heart of the work." It's an acceptance both of death and of anything else that might happen, like the magical appearance of a long-dead avatar to tell you that, yes, you are his true heir, you are the child he never had. And magic, as the British philosopher R. G. Collingwood wrote in 1937,

is a representation where the emotion evoked is an emotion evoked on account of its function in practical life . . . Magical activity is a kind of dynamo supplying the mechanism of practical life with the emotional current that drives it. Hence magic is a necessity for every sort and condition of men. A society which thinks, as ours thinks, that it has outlived the need for magic, is either mistaken in that opinion, or else it is a dying society, perishing for lack of interest in its own maintenance.

Which is a way of saying, with unusual repetitions kin to those that in Morrison's music always signify freedom, a love of words, and a lack of fear for what they might say ("the emotion evoked is an emotion evoked"), that to be born again might be understood as magic, magic as everyday life: what you do to preserve the emotional current that drives everyday life. And that current may be, in the art historian T. J. Clark's phrase, the sight of death—a sight that, when one is as attuned to contingency as the singer on *Astral Weeks* is, you see everywhere.

When Lewis Merenstein says the album "had to happen because it had to happen," that "if I would've gone somewhere else," not to Boston that day, the album "wouldn't have come out the way it did," or even taken any shape at all, he is situating the album as an event: a unique and timeless act or occurrence, like Bob Beamon's jump, something that could not have been predicted and could never be repeated. But that is only half of it. In "Astral Weeks," "Sweet Thing," "Cyprus Avenue," "Madame George," "Ballerina," and "Slim Slow Slider," there are everywhere in the music itself tiny events that are just as contingent; that single *hoyyyyyyyy* may be only the most immediately thrilling. These events take place in the breaks and holes in the music. They change what could have been a spot of dead air into a moment of anticipation. They turn the singer's claims into truth, the singer testing that truth with repetitions of a phrase until, now an incantation, not description, the phrase may have sloughed off all ordinary meaning and acquired one without intent or desire. It's the nearly countless "goodbye"s at the end of "Madame George" no longer necessarily signifying "fare thee well" or "I must take my leave" or "I'll never see you again" but "I'm returning," "I could never leave," "I will never forget you."

It's this sense of event within a song, a verse, a line, or even what might occur in the space between one word and another, that raises the cast of drama that hovers over the whole of the album. "I based the first fifteen minutes of *Taxi Driver* on *Astral Weeks*," Martin Scorsese said in 1978, just after the first major screening of his film *The Last Waltz*, sitting on the floor in his living room in the Hollywood hills, playing the album, hearing "Madame George" come up. "That's the song," he said—as in the moment Bernard Herrmann's theme for *Taxi Driver* played from inside of "Madame George," as "I Cover the Waterfront" played inside of that, and you could follow Travis Bickle, driving his hack from 6 P.M. to 6 A.M. every night, talking to himself, "All the animals come out at night, whores, skunk pussies, buggers, queens, fairies, dopers, junkies, sick, venal," as he drives under the spray of a broken hydrant and wishes for a rain that would wash all the sin off the streets, as he tries to talk up the ticket seller in a porn theater, as he sees his dream girl, describing her in his diary in words that could have come from "Sweet Thing": "She was wearing a white dress / She appeared like an angel / Out of this filthy mess."* It's all foreshadowing, as on *Astral Weeks* almost everything is memory, but the sense of tension is the same. Accompanying every shout of exaltation on *Astral Weeks*, every breath of comfort, there is a murmur of jeopardy and danger that makes you afraid for the people in the songs—afraid for Madame George, afraid for the singer who leaves her behind as if she's already dead, afraid that the singer so transformed by his self-raised specter of rebirth may not make it as far as, on the first track on *Astral Weeks*, its title song, he actually does. It's this that over the years has led so many people to take the album as a kind of talisman, to recognize

---

* It's *all* in "I Cover the Waterfront," as Morrison once recorded the song with John Lee Hooker—as Hooker, not Morrison, sings the standard as a ghost, back for another look, to make sure nothing has changed.

others by their affection for it, to say "I'm going to my grave with this record, I will never forget it."

"To this day it gives me pain to hear it," Merenstein said in 2009 of the record he produced, then pulling away from what he'd just said: "Pain is the wrong word—I'm so moved by it." But pain is exactly the right word: the pain, the fear, of knowing that to acknowledge that the music exists at all is to acknowledge that, because it might not have, it doesn't.

What lessons can it teach, what last words might it leave on anyone's lips? What does it say, where did it come from? In 2009, as Van Morrison was setting out to re-create *Astral Weeks* on stages around the world, with charts indicating every half-note, every caesura, every skipped beat, so that Jay Berliner and Richard Davis (who finally bowed out) could replay their parts exactly as they had more than forty years before, I was asked these questions, and I realized I didn't care. What happens on *Astral Weeks* beggars those questions. It was forty-six minutes in which possibilities of the medium—of rock 'n' roll, of pop music, of what you might call music that could be played on the radio as if it were both timeless and news—were realized, when you went out to the limits of what this form could do. You went past them: you showed everybody else that the limits they had accepted on invention, expression, honesty, daring, were false. You said it to musicians and you said it to people who weren't musicians: there's more to life than you thought. Life can be lived more deeply—with a greater sense of fear and horror and desire than you ever imagined.

That's what I heard at the time, and that's what I hear now. There is a difference. I no longer altogether trust the sort of explanations that along with other people I used to pursue so passionately—not, of course, philistine, literal explanations, of course not, but imaginative, contextualizing explanations that made both a work and its setting richer for the introduction of the one to the other. I've played *Astral Weeks* more than I've played any other record I own; I wouldn't tell you why even if I knew. In the face of work that became part of my life a long time ago and remains inseparable from it, whether it's *The Great Gatsby* or *Astral Weeks*, what I value most is how inexplicable any great work really is.

Dick Schaap, *The Perfect Jump* (New York: New American Library, 1976).

Hank Shteamer, "In Full: Lewis Merenstein, Producer of *Astral Weeks*," 3 March 2009, *Dark Forces Swing Blind Punches*, http://darkforcesswing.blogspot.com.

Barry Franklin, "Crawdaddy?" 1968, unpublished. Courtesy Barry Franklin.

Brooks Arthur, to Josh Gleason, "Van Morrison: *Astral Weeks* Revisited," *Weekend Edition*, NPR, 28 February 2009.

Jon Landau, "John Wesley Harding," *Crawdaddy!* May 1968, collected in *It's Too Late to Stop Now* (San Francisco: Straight Arrow Press, 1972), 52.

R. J. Collingwood, *The Principles of Art* (1937), quoted in Wilfred Mellers, *A Darker Shade of Pale: A Backdrop to Bob Dylan* (New York: Oxford, 1985), 33.

Lester Bangs, "Astral Weeks" (from *Stranded*, ed. GM, 1979), in Bangs, *Psychotic Reactions and Carburetor Dung*, ed. GM (New York: Knopf, 1987), 21, 20.

Martin Scorsese, to GM; see "Save the Last Waltz for Me," GM, *New West*, 22 May 1978, 95.

PiL (Public Image Ltd.), "Albatross," *Metal Box* (Virgin, 1979). Originally three twelve-inch 45s in a film can; the 1990 reissue was one CD in a four-and-three-quarter-inch tin: a PiL box.

Bob Dylan, "All Along the Watchtower," *John Wesley Harding* (Columbia, 1967).

Neil Young, "All Along the Watchtower," on *Bob Dylan 30th Anniversary Concert Celebration* (Columbia, 1993). A tribute show from Madison Square Garden, with, most notably, Johnny Winter on "Highway 61 Revisited," Roger McGuinn with Tom Petty and the Heartbreakers on "Mr. Tambourine Man," Lou Reed on "Foot of Pride," and Sinéad O'Connor on Bob Marley's "War" (leave it to her to break the rules), not to mention quite a few real stinkers.

Jimi Hendrix, "Star-Spangled Banner," on *Jimi Hendrix—Live at Woodstock* (MCA, 1999). The best account of what happened when Hendrix played the anthem is Jeff Bridges's Bob Dylan–written rant in the film *Masked and Anonymous*, dir. Larry Charles (Sony Pictures Classics, 2003). "I don't know, man. All I did was play it," Hendrix said on the *Dick Cavett Show* not long after Woodstock. "I'm American, so I played it. I used to sing it in school. They made me sing it in school, so it was a flashback." Cavett, as Michael Ventre reported in 2009 for MSNBC, "interrupted the interview to point out to the audience, 'This man was in the 101st Airborne, so when you send your nasty letters in . . .' Cavett then explained to Hendrix that whenever someone plays an 'unorthodox' version of the anthem, 'You immediately get a guaranteed percentage of hate mail.' Hendrix then respectfully disagreed with Cavett's description. 'I didn't think it was unorthodox,' he said. 'I thought it was beautiful.'"

John Lee Hooker, with Van Morrison, "I Cover the Waterfront," from *Mr. Lucky* (Virgin, 1991), included on the posthumous Hooker collection *The Best of Friends* (Shout! Factory, 2007), along with another Hooker-Morrison number, "Don't Look Back." The two also recorded "I'll Never Get Out of These Blues Alive" for Hooker's album of the same name (Crescendo, 1972), but the affinity was always personal, not musical. The laconic, reflective ethos Hooker brought to his music in his later years never really meshed with Morrison's instincts for the blues; no matter how he might have tried to keep it caged, urgency would almost always win out.

Van Morrison, *Astral Weeks* (Warner Bros.–Seven Arts, 1968).

——*Astral Weeks Live at the Hollywood Bowl* (Listen to the Lion, 2009).

ALMOST INDEPENDENCE DAY. 1972.
LISTEN TO THE LION. 1972.
CALEDONIA SOUL MUSIC. 1970

In 1972, Van Morrison closed each side of what might be his richest album, *St. Dominic's Preview*, with a song over ten minutes long.

One was "Almost Independence Day." Notes from Morrison's acoustic guitar twisted into a harsh minor key, then seemed to raise a flag as a skiff pushed off; a synthesizer made the sound of a tugboat pushing through fog, and kept it constant. As it went on, it seemed as if the song itself more than the singer was gazing out over San Francisco Bay to watch the fireworks; as that happened, the Fourth of July receded, and what was left was an unsettled, unclaimed, unfounded land where the event that settled it, named it, found it, had yet to take place.

The other long song was if anything stronger. "Listen to the Lion" was made as a field for the yarragh, an expanse over which, as a thing in itself, it could go wherever it might want to go, disappearing and reappearing at any time—but more than that "Listen to the Lion" was a song about the yarragh.

Writing about Morrison in 1978, Jonathan Cott quoted Yeats on the ancient Celts, living "in a world where anything might flow and change, and become any other thing . . . The hare that ran by among the dew might have sat up on his haunches when the first man was made, and the poor bunch of rushes under their feet might have been a goddess laughing among the stars; and with but a little magic, a little waving of the hands, a little murmuring of the lips, they too could become a hare or a bunch of rushes, and know immortal love and immortal hatred." With that little murmuring of the lips becoming a torrent of wind off a lake, after what appears to be a conventional song, though a particularly pious one ("I shall search my very soul . . . for the lion"), for one minute after another Morrison cries, moans, pleads, shouts, hollers, whispers, until finally he breaks with language and speaks in tongues, growling and rumbling. The feeling is that whoever it is that is singing has not simply abandoned language, but has returned himself to a time before language, and is now groping toward it. The organs of speech have not yet been fixed in the mouth and the throat, because there is no speech. Speech might come from the chest, the stomach, the bowels—and there, in a transporting minute, is where the singer seems to find it, guttural sounds now swirling and spinning around the singer in bodies of their own. "They too could become a hare"—now Morrison has loosed the lion inside himself.

As he sings, a chorus behind him urges him on, res-olutely, as if they understand the mission that the singer, caught in his trance, only senses. "Listen to the lion," they chant, drawing out the last word—but what is strange is that in the chorus, among three male voices, you hear Mor-rison himself, singing at himself.

As this happens they truly are two different, separate persons. It's more than, say, the conscious mind calling out to the subconscious; as the listener, you hear, you recog-nize, in a way that is tactile before it is anything else, two different bodies. "Listen to the lion," commands the chorus, but the singer already is the lion. *Awwrgh*, *arrgh*, *ooo*, *ah*, *ooo*, *mmm*, *ungh*, *ooo*, *ungh*, *arrgh*, *ah*, *ah*, off his feet in the dance—and then, not in exhaustion but with the clarity of a sudden change in the light, the singer removes his animal head to lead a fleet of ships. "And we sailed," he repeats five times, "away from Denmark, way up to Caledonia."

Caledonia is not just a misspelling of "Caldonia," a number-one race music hit for Louis Jordan and His Tym-pani Five in 1945 and a blues standard ever after—even if, purposefully misspelling the name, Morrison recorded a happily delirious version of the tune and put it out as a sin-gle in 1974, with his band credited as the Caledonia Soul Express: "CALDONIA! CALDONIA!" he shouted, as so many had before him, "*WHAT MAKES YOUR BIG HEAD SO HARD!*" No, Morrison will explain if you ask, as he

explained to Jonathan Cott, "Caledonia used to be Scotland.
This funny thing happened a long time ago—a lot of people
from Northern Ireland went over to Scotland to settle, and
vice versa. They changed spaces . . . So a lot of people from
Northern Ireland are of Scottish descent. And my name
suggests that I am."* But, Morrison would sometimes say,
there was more to it than that. In the early seventies, as he
tried to find a name for what he did, settling for a time on
"Caledonia soul music," he came upon the notion that finally the blues came not from Africa but from Scotland. The
true source of the blues was in the border ballads and folk
songs, from "The Cuckoo" to "Barbara Allen," from "She
Moves through the Fair" to "Nottamun Town," that, carried
by settlers from Britain to the Appalachians, made up the
oldest, deepest, and most persistent American music there
is—"Real American Music," as Emma Bell Miles, an edu-
cated, middle-class city lady turned mountain woman,
wrote in 1904 in *Harper's*. Thus, Morrison might whisper,
in a song or in an interview, he was always an American, just
as, his ancestors sailing from Scandinavia to Scotland, he

---

* "Well, actually it's Ulster Scots," Morrison said as he retraced the story
in 2009 in a conversation with Dave Marsh. "We're taught in school,
and also places in Europe—I don't know if they teach it in America—
the Scots were actually from Northern Ireland, originally. When they
went to Scotland, they called them Scots. It's the same people. And the
same people also later went back to Ulster. They were going back and
forth all the time. And at one point, the kingdom of Delradia was
Northern Ireland and the western part of Scotland—which was a kingdom unto itself. They're so close, Northern Ireland and Scotland—it's
so close, you can see it on a clear day."

was fated to become Irish. That here came from there, that
there are no separations, that all parts of himself and his
music are one. Picking up the notion from Morrison, Mark
Knopfler might have caught it best by throwing it away.
There's a Scottish piper and highland drums in his 2000
"What It Is," a heartbreakingly hard-boiled history lesson—
when he bends the line "The ghost of Dirty Dick is still in
search of Little Nell" against a thief-in-the-night fiddle part,
it breaks my heart, anyway—and buried in Knopfler's mut-
tering is "the Caledonian blues." When in 1970, at the heart
of *Moondance*, the album that brought Morrison an audience that would stay with him, he let the words "Ere the
bonnie boat was won / As we sailed into the mystic" float
the music, this might have been what he meant.

The most remarkable aspect of this crackpot theory is
that it might be true. Certainly that is how the Virginia
novelist Sharyn McCrumb sees it. "The first Appalachian
journey," she writes, citing the geologist Kevin Dann's
1988 study *Traces on the Appalachians: A History of Serpentine in the Americas*, "was the one made by the mountains
themselves."

The proof of this can be found in a vein of a green mineral called
serpentine which forms its own subterranean "Appalachian Trail"
along America's eastern mountains, stretching from north Georgia
to the hills of Nova Scotia, where it seems to stop. This same vein of
serpentine can be found in the mountains of western Ireland, where
it again stretches into Cornwall, Wales, Scotland, and the Orkneys,
finally ending in the Arctic Circle. More than two hundred and fifty

million years ago the mountains of Appalachia and the mountains of Great Britain fit together like a jigsaw puzzle. Continental drift pulled them apart, at the same time it formed the Atlantic Ocean.

The mountains' family connection to Britain reinforced what I had felt about the migration patterns of the early settlers. People forced to leave a land they loved come to America. Hating the flat, crowded eastern seaboard, they head westward on the Wilderness Road until they reach the wall of mountains. They follow the valleys south-southwest down through Pennsylvania, and finally find a place where the ridges rise, where you can see vistas of mountains across the valley. The Scots, the Irish, the Welsh, the Cornishmen— all those who had lives along the other end of the serpentine chain— to them this place must have looked right. Must have felt right. Like home. *And they were right back in the same mountains they had left behind in Britain.*

"Caledonia Soul Music," an eighteen-minute piece recorded in 1970, passed on to the FM station KSAN in San Francisco, played often, and never released, can contain all of that without distortion. With almost no words, it is all suggestion, and the music is so bottomless that any words one might bring to it from somewhere else can seem true, just as the right melody, the right voice, can make banal lyrics seem unbearably profound. It's the most complete and in a way the most modest statement of Morrison's music: as if there were, somewhere, a form to which all of his best work aspired, a form that could never be realized, except that this time it was.

Here Morrison is a bandleader, not a singer. Really his role is as a conductor, but he appears more as a pathfinder, issuing directions under his breath, his mission to lead everyone out of the forest and into the light, except that sometimes the light in the forest is too much to turn away from, and so as a pathfinder he tries to get the band lost. Thus after stolidly announcing the title as acoustic guitar, bass, and piano slowly open the theme, a mandolin behind them hinting at a story that for the time being will be untold, Morrison lets his lips murmur, and you can think he's building up to words to sing. He isn't. There's a sigh: *Yeah*. They have all night.

"Only rarely onstage do bands achieve reality," David Thomas, the leader of Pere Ubu, the Cleveland band that in 1975 set out to find what, it seemed to them, no one else was looking for, once said. "Mostly it's in rehearsals, in lost moments." As with the Beatles in 1969, chasing all over the room for songs that were running from them like mice as they tried to make the album that would appear as *Let It Be*, seizing for a moment on Buddy Holly—after all, hadn't they named themselves for his Crickets? It's a mess, one stumble after another, and then John Lennon finds "Maybe Baby." "We used to do it," he says pathetically, as if there's no chance they could do it now. George Harrison follows, and there's an explosion of longing and loss, and now one song is another, there are no borders, they're rolling in the meadows of melody, no difference at all between "Peggy Sue Got Married" and "Crying, Waiting, Hoping"—and then Lennon moves into "Mailman Bring Me No More Blues" and the rhythm is fixed, the others lock in behind him, the progression is firm, the words are clear, and all the life is gone. It's like Dana Wynter turning her face to Kevin

McCarthy at the end of *Invasion of the Body Snatchers* just after she's gone over to the other side.

The reality that the Beatles found for a few unshaped, indelible seconds is what Morrison sustains for eighteen minutes. As he says softly every time the piece seems about to run away from itself, "Take it . . . take it slow," he could be shaking hands with Morton Feldman, the composer complaining that no matter how quietly anyone tried to play his music it was still "too fuckin' loud and too fuckin' fast." Here Morrison is at once composer and audience. As the composer he knows what he wants, but as the audience he knows that when the composer knows where he or she wants to go but the musicians don't, anything can happen, and what might happen can go beyond anyone's intentions. So at the center of his circle of musicians, Morrison waits. At times the band is as bent on finality as the Rolling Stones in their 1966 "Going Home," an ordinary three-minute song that turned into eleven minutes that were never repeated; then Morrison takes them to the point where the idea of an ending makes no sense. "Get some horn," Morrison might say, making the three words into a song in itself, and then from a saxophone comes a sound so warm you regret the fact that it will go away even as you grasp for it.

"You got it," Morrison says. Everywhere, pieces of music are hiding within the foreground sound, stepping out at any time. The drift of the music, a sort of nineteenth-century campfire lullaby, a crew looking for the headwaters of the Ohio but for a night allowing the music to let them believe they've already found it, is so complete that when in a flat, dumbly unmusical voice Morrison announces that "John will play a taste of mandolin" (*The kitchen will close in ten minutes*) it sounds like a joke on the credulousness of the musicians themselves: *Can you believe it? They thought I was serious!* But John Platania takes up the cue, quietly ringing out a calm, head-down progression over drums, bass, a bare piano, a spectral saxophone, as Morrison mutters and hums—and then, perhaps two minutes in, he hits what is almost a discord and the notes lift in volume. "*Ahhhhh!*" Morrison responds, involuntarily, as pure reflex, feeling the music in his stomach, the yarragh as pure pleasure.

There's a way everything he did before this moment was to reach the point where as a musician who is also a listener, he would find that sound, and everything he has done since an attempt to find it again.

Jonathan Cott, "Van Morrison: The *Rolling Stone* Interview," *Rolling Stone*, 30 November 1978, 51, 54.

Sharyn McCrumb, "A Novelist Looks at the Land," *Appalachian Voice*, Late Winter 2005.

"Only rarely do bands": David Thomas to GM, 17 February 1998.

Mark Knopfler, "What It Is," on *Sailing to Philadelphia* (WEA/Reprise, 2000).

Beatles, "Maybe Baby," et al. Devin McKinney: "State of the art bootleg versions are on Disc 4 of the January 29 [1969] installment of A/B Road, the 83-disc collection of Get Back sessions from Purple Chick (2004)." So there.

Van Morrison, "Almost Independence Day" and "Listen to the Lion," on *St. Dominic's Preview* (Warner Bros., 1972).

————with the Caledonia Soul Express, "Caledonia" (Warner Bros., 1974), included on *Catalog Strays 1965–2000* (Wild Card bootleg).

————"Caledonia Soul Music," included on *No Stone Unturned* (Head bootleg).

MOONSHINE WHISKEY. 1971

It's the way he affirms "I'm gonna put on my hot pants" as if he's trying to twist himself into them. But were they pink?

Van Morrison, "Moonshine Whiskey," on *Tupelo Honey* (Warner Bros., 1971).

JUST LIKE A WOMAN. 1971

It's an affront, this performance—to the song if not the songwriter. And where does someone get the nerve to take on a song like this?

In 1966, on Bob Dylan's *Blonde on Blonde*, the arrangement was a web, a cocoon for the singer. The more he filled in the story, the hazier it became. The touch was soft, the music sweet. By the end, it didn't matter if knowledge won out over regret. The final "I / Just can't fit" was a sad wave goodbye. It was a great make-out song.

By 1971, when Van Morrison and his Caledonia Soul Orchestra went into Wally Heider's Pacific High Studios in San Francisco to play a show for a live broadcast on KSAN, the Bay Area's leading independent contemporary music station, he was a hometown star. The year before, having flown in for a show from his home in Woodstock, he'd spent a day driving from San Francisco to Marin County to

Berkeley and back to San Francisco; the radio was on and
he was all over it. Just as "Gloria" dominated the AM airwaves in the Bay Area in 1965—the next year the local Top
40 station KFRC held a poll to determine the three hundred greatest records of all time (the previous fifteen years),
and "Gloria" was in the top ten along with the Rolling
Stones' "(I Can't Get No) Satisfaction," the Righteous
Brothers' "You've Lost That Lovin' Feeling," the Byrds' "Mr.
Tambourine Man," Bob Dylan's "Like a Rolling Stone," and
two versions of "Louie Louie"—by 1970 Morrison, an indistinct name almost everywhere else, probably got more
airplay on KSAN than anyone else. "Madame George."
"Brown-Eyed Girl." "T. B. Sheets." "Here Comes the Night."
Practically everything from the 1970 *Moondance*, except for
the TV-commercial jazz of the title song: "Come Running,"
"Caravan," "Crazy Love," "Into the Mystic," "Brand New
Day," "Glad Tidings." All in an afternoon. You could almost
see the lightbulb going on over Morrison's head.

In 1968, Morrison married a Bay Area native who called
herself Janet Planet and moved with her from Cambridge
to Woodstock—as she would say later, to meet Bob Dylan.
Morrison, she said, considered him his only peer. Now
Morrison had a home in Marin County. Nationally his albums were charting in the high twenties or low thirties;
here he was number one. He could do no wrong.

That night in San Francisco, with an audience in the
studio, he sang Woody Guthrie's "Dead or Alive." He sang
"Hound Dog" and Sam Cooke's "Bring It On Home to Me"
and Fats Domino's "Blue Monday" along with songs from

Moondance and the new *Tupelo Honey*. He sang "Friday's Child," an all but unknown song he'd recorded with Them. All in all it was a happy night, which made the perversity of Morrison's "Just Like a Woman" that much more stark.

With Dylan's original the music is like a wheel. With every break between chorus and verse the song returns to its beginning, and a feeling of calm settles over the traumas the people in the song have already left behind. It's not just a great make-out song: at the end, when the singer imagines himself and his old lover meeting again, at some party where nobody knows what they once were to each other, it's a seduction song. "You break just like a little girl." Oh! No one understands me like you do!

All of that is stripped away when Morrison starts in on the tune. He takes the first lines flatly, simply, as if he has too much respect for the words to sing them. The backing—guitar, piano, light drums—is perfunctory, until it's stiff, its stiffness soon enough turning hackneyed, with Morrison using the instruments as one to smash down after each word of the chorus:

And she! *wham* Makes! *wham* Love! *wham*

There are melodramatic touches, as in almost any TV drama or bad movie where any important phrase is paused and repeated—*No matter what happens, I'll be there for you—I'll be there for you*, except that here it's "Queen Mary, she's, she's my friend," or "It was your, your world"—all but semaphore flags to alert the audience that something terribly important is being said, to drive home the actor's or the singer's sincerity, to the point that any phrase that might smell of portentousness is guaranteed to perfume the room.

Is it all a setup, a man casing a joint in respectable clothes because tomorrow he's going to rob it blind? That's a question the performance refuses to answer; you have to answer it yourself. As Morrison moves into the second verse

> It was raining from the first
> And I was dying of thirst

he seems even more stolid than before. He could be giving a speech. The band is still merely following along, the piano perhaps slightly brighter than before. But then the pianist adds a triplet, and the music exerts the smallest pull on the singer. You might not even notice—but unconsciously, your memory registers the moment. There's a shift—

> And your long-time curse hurts but what
>   is worse
> Is this pain in here

—and there's a lilt in the last phase, an opening to

> I can't remain in here

and as you feel Morrison draw a breath you feel the band rush forward to draw it for him—

> I can't stay in here

—the "stay" shredding in his mouth as the words are blown out of their own song by a scream that is somehow more controlled, more melodic, than anything before, the melody now armed with passion behind it or the fright it creates

AIN'T IT CLEAR

and you feel that nothing could rise higher than this fire until the next word does, and the next word is "I," five times, not repeated but each exploding syllable modulated into the next until it is all one unholy word, a plea the singer is addressing to himself. What just happened? Is there anybody left alive?

And then, in the most perverse gesture of all, Morrison produces the next lines, again flatly, as if he could care less. He ornaments a phrase with that TV-script repetition that mocks you for buying the phony emotion behind the delivery in the first place

I believe I believe I believe I believe I believe
it's time for us to

and so floridly that when he finishes with a curt

Quit.

there really is a period after the word.

And then he does it all again. You want to say you won't be fooled this time, but you are. After the song is blown apart for the second time, you want him to say he meant every ache, every cut, but he doesn't.

He does get out of the song in a way that humanizes what he's done, that puts the singer in the song, for the first time one of its characters, not its assassin: "You were weird, and I was weird, too." You play the song again, trying to make it happen as your own heart has played it.

Bob Dylan, "Just Like a Woman," on *Blonde on Blonde* (Columbia, 1966).

Van Morrison, "Just Like a Woman," on *The Inner Mystic: Recorded Live at Pacific High Studios*, California, September 1971, as broadcast on KSAN-FM, San Francisco (Oh Boy/Odyssey bootleg).

Janet Planet, see Michael Gray, *Bob Dylan Encyclopedia* (New York: Continuum, 2006), 465.

THE LAST LAUGH, ON MARK KNOPFLER,
SAILING TO PHILADELPHIA. 2000

Ever since Dire Straits' "Sultans of Swing," his first record and a worldwide hit, Mark Knopfler has had a touch. Usually it's the ability to find a doomy, fatalistic melody and let it send a man who gives off the feeling of someone who never stops looking over his shoulder down the street. When it works—on "Romeo and Juliet" and "Wild West End" on Dire Straits' 1980 *Making Movies*, or the single "What It Is," from *Sailing to Philadelphia*—you could be walking in the footsteps of Michael Caine's Jack Carter.

Anyone who bought *Sailing to Philadelphia* hoping for more of what he or she was hearing on the radio was not going to be happy. It was a famous-names showcase, and the first thing that caught your ear was James Taylor on the title song, in his wounded-puppy "You've Got a Friend" mode. Elsewhere there were the Christian pop singers Chris

Rodriquez and Tim Davis, the Americana duo Gillian
Welch and David Rawlings, and Glenn Tilbrook and Chris
Difford of the once-wonderful British pop group Squeeze.

The first four songs on the album were so bland you
could forget you were listening to it. The first verse of "The
Last Laugh," crooned by Knopfler, was no different. And
then, one minute into the song, there was Van Morrison.

A single word—the "learned" in "Games you thought
you'd learned"—is enough to take you off the record, into a
country whose only maps are in Morrison's pockets. This is a
place made of regret, where the deepest impulse is to return
to the scene of the crime, so everything can be made right. If
you can't do that, can't you sing a song that the person you
wounded might hear, and wouldn't that be almost as good?
But what if the wrong was done to you, by someone who
likely hasn't thought of you since? If that person heard you,
coming out of a radio they didn't turn off because they like
Mark Knopfler, would anything happen in their heart?

Knopfler's song itself is nothing—but all of these questions are put into the air as Morrison draws them from his
chest. It's not that so much is being expressed; it's that the
fullness of Morrison's voice as he steps up to the song immediately erases the limits that Knopfler himself has already established as to what could be expressed. Now the possibility
that anything could be said hangs in the air. It's not a singer's
trick; it doesn't always happen when Morrison steps through
someone else's door. On the Chieftains' 1995 *The Long Black
Veil*—featuring Mick Jagger on the title song with a voice that
a resident of a certain mountain county in Virginia claims

can be traced to just that place, Sinéad O'Connor on "The Foggy Dew" and "She Moved Through the Fair," Marianne Faithfull on the ancient "Love Is Teasin'," Tom Jones on "The Tennessee Waltz," and for that matter Mark Knopfler on "Lily of the West"— Morrison has nothing to offer "Have I Told You Lately That I Love You" other than to reveal how little the song might tell a singer. In Mike Figgis's 2003 film *Red, White & Blues*, about the British blues world, Morrison raises his guitar and launches into "Rambler's Blues." Formally he's masterful; he's also scholastic, more writing about the song than singing it, and his writing misses the song. Tom Jones hovers in the background; after a minute or so you wish he'd open his mouth and take the song away.

There's no saying why in "The Last Laugh" Morrison finds a story to tell. Maybe he heard someone had to save the song, even if he hadn't yet heard if it was worth it. Maybe it was the line "You've neither lost or won" or simply "Out on the highway," which opens into that whole country, and suddenly the whole song is bigger, fuller, wanting more from Knopfler, as he moves into a guitar solo, than he can give, and more from the listener.

One of those things: you put a man next to a microphone, hand him a sheet of words, and soul comes out.

Mark Knopfler, "The Last Laugh," *Sailing to Philadelphia* (Warner Bros., 2000).

The Chieftains, *The Long Black Veil* (BMG, 1995).

Van Morrison, "Rambler's Blues," in Mike Figgis, *Martin Scorsese Presents the Blues: Red, White & Blues* (Hip-O, 2003).

PART THREE

A BELIEF IN THE BLUES AS A KIND OF CURSE ONE PUTS ON ONESELF

COMMON ONE. 1980.
BEAUTIFUL VISION. 1982.
INARTICULATE SPEECH OF THE HEART. 1983.
LIVE AT THE GRAND OPERA HOUSE BELFAST. 1984.
A SENSE OF WONDER. 1984.
NO GURU, NO METHOD, NO TEACHER. 1986.
POETIC CHAMPIONS COMPOSE. 1987.
IRISH HEARTBEAT, WITH THE CHIEFTAINS. 1988.
AVALON SUNSET. 1989.
ENLIGHTENMENT. 1990.
HYMNS TO THE SILENCE. 1991.
TOO LONG IN EXILE. 1993.
A NIGHT IN SAN FRANCISCO. 1994.
DAYS LIKE THIS. 1995.
HOW LONG HAS THIS BEEN GOING ON. 1996
TELL ME SOMETHING. 1996

How do you write off more than fifteen albums and more than fifteen years of the work of a great artist? You might do the same with Bob Dylan's records from *Street Legal* in 1978 right up to the bend in the road of *Good As I Been to You* in 1992—or I might, anyway, remembering how everything from *Slow Train Coming* to *Infidels* to *Empire Burlesque* to *Knocked Out Loaded* to *Down in the Groove* to *Oh Mercy* to *Under the Red Sky* was marked by a *Rolling Stone* review celebrating it as *yes, finally, not like the last one, this is the real comeback!* and with the actual turn toward something crawlingly alive missed for the lack of a signpost. But that was a singer who for a long time had nothing to sing about. Something different was happening with Van Morrison.

"What defines great singing in the rock and soul era," Jonathan Lethem wrote in 2008, "is some underlying tension in the space between singer and song. A bridge is being built across that void, and it's a bridge we're never sure the singer's going to manage to cross. The gulf may reside between vocal texture and the actual meaning of the words, or between the singer and the band, the musical genre, the style of production, what have you . . . " But what if there is no tension—not because the singer has momentarily lost it, but because his goal has been to transcend it, and he's succeeded?

In 1975 I found myself passing the road leading to Van Morrison's Marin County house; it was posted with a sign reading "Van Morrison Self-Improvement Camp." He was working on it at the time. His career remained a kind of war, with producers, managers, himself. His music was a Möbius strip: no new work had ever made his past work inaccessible; none of his best work had caused anything else to sound dated or immature. His mistakes didn't subvert the shape of his story, because scars and wounds were part of it. He might stand still on stage, but you never knew where you, as part of the audience, stood with him, or vice versa. His relationship to the audience seemed somehow accidental, or worse. There was a show in Berkeley in 1973 that began with cutting versions of Morrison's own "St. Dominic's Preview," Sonny Boy Williamson's "Help Me," and Muddy Waters's "I Just Want to Make Love to You," and then careened out of control. Morrison had been standing in a dim blue light—not bright enough to see his face, but bright enough to see he had one. He broke off the Waters song and ordered "the spotlight" out. He didn't have his shades, he said. He wasn't in L.A., whatever that meant. He continued in complete darkness. It seemed appropriate— mercurial weirdness was part of his appeal. But out of the dark came a throwaway version of "Listen to the Lion," a flat "Caravan," and then the announcement of the last song: "Misty." "As I wander through this garbage world alone," Morrison sang, leaving the garbage world—the audience—alone.

God knows it was a memorable show. There was nothing obvious about it. Lethem's bridge came into view, suspense over whether Morrison might cross it grew, he didn't cross it, and that failure stuck more than the triumphs of countless other good performers, who leave you feeling you've seen something unforgettable, something you can hardly remember a week later. Morrison's resistance to an audience in those years was palpable, so concrete you could feel it pressing on your chest, as if to say, *Where is it written*

that just because I want to come out on stage with the musi-
cians I trust and take my songs where they've never been be-
fore there has to be someone there to watch?

At a show in San Francisco in 1978, Morrison encored
with "Caravan." He opened up space in the song, as if daring the crowd to anticipate his timing. He'd done this sort
of thing for years, perhaps most shockingly in a passage
captured on " . . . *It's Too Late to Stop Now* . . . ," his first live
album, recorded in 1973 in a nightclub in Los Angeles and
a theater in London. The last number—on a double album
that unfolded like a single show—was "Cyprus Avenue,"
from *Astral Weeks*. Morrison used a stop-time beat, allowing for long pauses between lines, spaces where he could
try anything, crossroads where he could take the song in
any direction. Inside the story of the song, the singer
watched all the fourteen-year-old girls parading down the
street on their way home from school: "And the leaves fall
one by one by one by one by one by one by one by one—on
the hometown fool." He looks at one of the girls, the one
he's waited for. He thinks about what he wants to do to her.
He makes no move to cross the street, to approach her, to
speak to her, but he can't help thinking about speaking to
her, and as soon as he does think about it, he freezes. "And
my tongue gets tied" is what he sang when he recorded the
song. But that's too easy. Now it's "And my tongue gets t—,
t—"—and the act is so convincing, the break in the song so
violent, the drawbridge opening so that the only way to
cross it is to back up, floor the accelerator, and pray, that
the whole show is sucked into the suspended moment. It's

as if there's no way out—in the instant, you might be plunged back into memories of the times you sat nervously with a stuttering friend, and how you ached with everything you had for him to get the word he was trying to say out of his mouth, to the point where you could see yourself reaching your hand down his throat and grabbing it. Onstage, someone in the band makes a cheek-popping sound, right on the beat. There's nervous laughter in the crowd. A saxophone seems to walk around the stage, and you can imagine the player circling the singer, pointing at him, as if to ensure that no one misses his humiliation, which he can't escape. "It's too late to stop now!" are the triumphant last words of the show, but right now the singer can't stop and he'd give anything if he could. "Every time I try to speak," he wants to say, but it comes out "Evry tam, tr—, tr—, sp—" The saxophone stutters, the piano hits random notes, "Every," he tries again. It comes out "errry," and then, as it happens in real life, the curse is lifted: "And my insides shake," clear and smooth, and then a rush, as if to outrun the stutter that only pauses to take a breath: "Justlikealeaf-onatree." The whole crisis lasts barely more than twenty seconds, but while it's happening it feels like a trap you'll never get out of.

At the show in San Francisco five years later, in the midst of "Caravan," the stops in the music, the seemingly atonal, irrational bursts and jerks, were as dramatic and disconcerting as they were in that "Cyprus Avenue"; instead of titters, shouts, or even heckling, the crowd responded with unison clapping, as if to stop the music altogether, or

force it back into a regular time. For the first time that
night, save for an introduction of the band, Morrison
spoke to the crowd. "Just shut up," he said. "Just shut up.
We do the work here, not you."

That was the highlight of the show. In some ways, looking forward, now, to the years that would follow, it was pre-
dictive, an acting out of things to come, because otherwise
there was no tension in the show at all. It was formal. Everything was pitched to a middle range: desire and pleasure,
never joy or rage. The band held strictly to arrangements,
giving Morrison nothing to sing against. The people in the
audience were pushing harder than the people on the stage.

Outside of that strange "Caravan," what Morrison was
offering, as he turned songs over to background singers,
pressed each number into a single dimension, and sang at
his songs rather than from inside of them, was one true
side of himself as a performer: the romantic of "Tupelo
Honey," the person who makes music of affection, sensual-
ity, and acceptance. He wants peace of mind and ordered
satisfaction most of all, and sings as if he already has them.
But the singer who by 1978 had already caused some
people to commit themselves to his music as if it was their
quest as well as his had won them because of his distrust of
conventional satisfactions and his inability to rest with any
sort of peace. This was the person behind "Listen to the
Lion" and "Mystic Eyes." What he wants most is freedom,
and what he has to say is that getting hold of freedom is
perhaps not as hard as living up to it, standing up to it.
When both sides of Morrison's music come together, the

result can be a sort of mystical deliverance. The listener is spared not a single fear, but he or she is somehow insulated from all fears—as is the performer. This is what happens on *Astral Weeks*, in "Almost Independence Day," in the wild shrieks of the steel guitar on "St. Dominic's Preview," or the insistent fetishism of windowsill, letter box, door, and backstreet jellyroll—*No, you don't take off the left shoe first, you take off the* right *shoe!*—in "And the Healing Has Begun." But when only one side of the conflict is presented, one is only too aware of what is being held back—and what is held back will find its way out one way or the other, as it did this night, when Van the orderly romantic told his audience to shut up.

Perhaps the real harbinger of what was to come came with "Help Me." "I've transcended myself," Morrison shouted at one point; here he was back in the pit, switching back and forth between his harmonica and the words of the song, long, harsh, overblown, pure sleazy 1967 Fillmore Auditorium white blues but the feeling of blood on the floor just the same, like Dennis Hopper reciting Roy Orbison's rewrite of the song, "In Dreams," in *Blue Velvet* ("In dreams—I *walk* with you—In dreams—I talk—to *you*"): "When you walk, walk with me—when you talk, talk with me! You gotta help me—I can't do it all by myself!" Morrison wasn't asking the crowd for encouragement, as most singers would do with this song—just as Dennis Hopper's Frank couldn't have cared less what Kyle MacLachan's Jeffrey made of what he was spewing in his face. Morrison's plea was aimed at someone, or something, much harder to reach.

Over the next fifteen years, that plea would be almost constant—a hole in the nearly seamless fabric opening up with the fatalism of "Raglan Road" on *Irish Heartbeat*, all sides of Morrison's music coming together as if in the ultimate and yet transcendently raceless minstrel show of *A Night in San Francisco*, John Lee Hooker, Georgie Fame, the bluesmen Junior Wells and Jimmy Witherspoon, the saxophonist Candy Dulfer, and Morrison's own daughter Shana Morrison along for the ride. The romantic would be replaced by the seeker, and the seeker would replace the anti-romantic's refusal of an audience with an insistence that no one be permitted to miss the point. You couldn't tell religion from therapy. "Were you healed tonight?" someone shouts to the crowd as the last number on *A Night in San Francisco* railed to a close—it was "Gloria" pulled out of Johnny Kidd and the Pirates' 1960 "Shakin' All Over," perhaps the first true British rock 'n' roll hit, as if by cesarean section.

As a soul man Morrison had been a lyric poet; he could suggest Yeats. In 1980, on *Common One*, he began to insist on the connection, which meant the songs didn't remotely suggest it. With two of the six numbers passing by at more than fifteen minutes—by far the longest pieces he'd ever released—Morrison had time to claim his roots; he pretty much had time to research them, write up his findings, publish them in a book, and watch it go out of print. Instead he name dropped. "Yeats and Lady Gregory corresponded, corresponded, corresponded"—his familiar obsessive repetition no longer changing the shape of the words, making them speak in new tongues, but telling you Yeats and Lady Gregory wrote a lot of letters. "James Joyce wrote streams of consciousness books." "Did you ever hear about Wordsworth and Coleridge? Did you ever hear about William Blake?"

Since as a lyric poet, or even a lyric poetaster, Morrison was a soul man, this shouldn't have mattered. In 1974, on the hypnotizing "You Don't Pull No Punches, But You Don't Push the River," Morrison was searching for the Veedon Fleece—what he named the album the song came from—and no one has ever figured out what that was.* The Veedon Fleece seemed to float above the churning music, which soon enough—a lift from an acoustic guitar, a piano thinking it over even as the boat is untied, drums on the offbeat, a flute as second mind, strings as a single rhythm instrument—was that river itself. There was a feeling caught in *Once Upon a Time in the West*, not even the movie, merely the title; suspense rose like a cloud. "The real soul people, the real soul people," Morrison chanted, pointing toward "the west coast," though he didn't say of what; as he summoned William Blake and the Eternals they were a band, just as the Sisters of Mercy he called for would become one, and together they sought the Veedon Fleece, but now the bridge was underwater, every shape shifting as you

---

* In 1974, just as he was about to release the record, Morrison went on KSAN in San Francisco to promote it. "The album's called *Veedon Fleece*," he said. "V-E-E-D-O-N F-L-E-E-C-E. And it doesn't, it means, ah"—and at just that instant there was a huge burst of static. He might have been saying "it means what it says," but I wouldn't bet on it.

tried to see your way to the bottom. The nearly nine minutes of the song went by like wind.

On *Common One*, as on so many of the albums to follow, the singing was so characterless and the sax-and-trumpet ensemble playing so faceless that the mention of a famous name became an event, something to hang on to—as it would be for so long for someone with nothing to say and an infinite commitment to getting it across. The tedium was almost heroic in its refusal to quit.

Near the end of "You Don't Pull No Punches, But You Don't Push the River," the music loosens to the point that it begins to break up, its elements separating. The song isn't falling apart—each part is moving off as a song in itself. You don't know where the song is. Strings shake, giving off the long horn of a storm warning, a yarragh if anything is. But for all Morrison returned to this river between 1980 and 1996 it could have had corpses floating on it. Even from a bridge you wouldn't want to look.

Jonathan Lethem, "The Fly in the Ointment," collected in *Best Music Writing 2009*, ed. GM (New York: Da Capo, 2009), 186–187.

Van Morrison, "Cyprus Avenue," on *". . . It's Too Late to Stop Now . . ."* (Warner Bros., 1974).

————"You Don't Pull No Punches, But You Don't Push the River," on *Veedon Fleece* (Warner Bros., 1974).

————*Common One* (Warner Bros., 1980).

————*Beautiful Vision* (Warner Bros., 1982).

————*Inarticulate Speech of the Heart* (Warner Bros., 1983).

————*Live at the Grand Opera House Belfast* (Mercury, 1984).

————*A Sense of Wonder* (Mercury, 1984).

————*No Guru, No Method, No Teacher* (Mercury, 1986).

————*Poetic Champions Compose* (Mercury, 1987).

————and the Chieftains, *Irish Heartbeat* (Mercury, 1988).

————*Avalon Sunset* (Polydor, 1989).

————*Enlightenment* (Mercury, 1990).

————*Hymns to the Silence* (Polydor, 1991).

————*Too Long in Exile* (Polydor, 1993).

————*A Night in San Francisco* (Polydor, 1994).

————*Days Like This* (Polydor, 1995).

————with Georgie Fame & friends, *How Long Has This Been Going On* (Verve, 1996).

————*Tell Me Something: The Songs of Mose Allison* (Verve, 1996).

LINDEN ARDEN STOLE THE HIGHLIGHTS. 1974

"Do you hear that? That's a prayer," Jonathan Cott said to me as we listened to the second cut on Van Morrison's 1974 *Veedon Fleece*. The first song, "Fair Play for You," a harmlessly slow reverie, was no preparation.

What Cott was talking about was the piano piece that opens "Linden Arden Stole the Highlights." It seemed to begin and end the song—to be utterly complete in itself—before Morrison sang his first word. I'm not sure what I heard that day—I remember saying *Yes, yes*, as if Cott had unlocked the song, and so fully it didn't matter whatever "Linden Arden Stole the Highlights" meant. What I hear now is a long series of earned wishes, the plea—if it's a prayer, it's the Platters'—of someone who knows what he or she wants, knows what he or she deserves, has little or no expectation of getting any of it, and who is absolutely at peace with such a life, or such an ending. The knowledge is enough. I don't hear a door anymore; I hear a pool that you dive into simply by listening.

There's no need to come up. I didn't catch the words that day, or for years to come. It didn't occur to me that the song needed them—or maybe it was that even as Morrison sang the words, the song itself forgot them.

As Morrison slides back and forth along the planes of the melody, as if he were a drop of mercury and someone were tilting a hand mirror now up, now down, he slides past the literal story he's telling—a crime story, as it turns out—into a tale of thought, dream, desire, where the claims of each shift in primacy. Passion rises and his voice fills up, and you are in the moment, but when Morrison lets his voice fade, as if he can hardly bear to listen to himself, because the thought he's trying to bring into view is so elusive the act of listening will break it, there is the feeling of someone looking back at himself from a future that has itself already passed. This is a greater kind of slowness. Whatever movement the music makes, it also pulls against itself: *not yet*.

It was hundreds of listenings to this song later, decades after listening to it with Cott, that, driving in a car, the radio on, I heard the story the song was carrying—I can't say, *about*. With a speaker a few inches from your face, words come across like traffic reports: out of the Druidic forest of the music comes a killer. Other killers track him from Ireland to a bar in San Francisco. He faces them down and kills them all. Dirty Harry straight off the boat.

The pool is always there, though. What happens in those first seconds with the piano, then in the way Morrison high-steps across an arc in the melody that has only just appeared to carry the listener across the first line, "Linden Arden stole the highlights"—if that was his crime, what kind of crime is that? When you kill someone, do you not simply put out their lights but take them?—returns the song at any time from its words to its music, the words remaining only as a signifier that a particular person is singing the song.

It's the quieting of the music that's uncanny. With Robert Johnson's "Stones in My Passway"—the kind of deep blues, constructed with an art so realized it conceals itself, that's one source of "Linden Arden Stole the Highlights"— there's nothing you can do to quiet it. The more you turn the volume down, the more the irreducible loudness of the song, its nightmare desolation and fright, creeps forward. But with "Linden Arden Stole the Highlights," the louder you try to make it, the more it recedes, until it reaches as far as it will go toward silence, making you lean into it.

When the Miracles' "The Love I Saw in You Was Just a Mirage" appeared in 1967, it radiated a sublimity that made everything that surrounded it on the radio sound faintly obscene. This song can do the same to whatever you happened to be doing with your life before you heard it, for the first time or the thousandth. Whether that is art ennobling life or corrupting it I don't know.

Robert Johnson, "Stones in My Passway" (1937), collected on *Robert Johnson—The Complete Recordings* (Columbia, 1990).

Smokey Robinson and the Miracles, "The Love I Saw in You Was
  Just a Mirage" (Tamla, 1967).
Van Morrison, "Linden Arden Stole the Highlights," on *Veedon
  Fleece* (Warner Bros., 1974).

BREAKFAST ON PLUTO. 2005

In Neil Jordan's 2005 film *Breakfast on Pluto*, the young transvestite Kitten, who was raised with the name Patrick Braden, has left her hometown in Ireland to find the mother who abandoned her at birth: "She went to London, the biggest city in the world," Kitten says to anyone she meets, "and it swallowed her up." But now Kitten has discovered where her mother lives. Flamboyant, shrieking, weepy, yet with the self-possession of someone with an infinite sense of irony, she sits in the dressing room of the Soho peep show where she works, surrounded by women from the club. She's wearing a short blond curly wig and a demure suit, applying light makeup, speaking in a quiet, careful voice; a folded newspaper propped up against the mirror, with a laughing photo of Margaret Thatcher and the head-line "VICTORY," tells us the year is 1979. Then we see the movement of an escalator, with people emerging from a tube station, and as Kitten's face comes into view Van Morrison's "Madame George," from eleven years before the historical moment of the film, creeps almost imperceptibly onto the soundtrack. It sounded like an invocation loosed from time when it first appeared, and it does now.

Breakfast on Pluto floats on a sea of music—a sea wide enough to make plain both the world in which Van Morrison has since the mid-1960s done his work, and how different and deep that work has been. A product of the ear as much as the eye, the film opens with "Sugar Baby Love," a 1974 hit by the made-up group the Rubettes—a delirious producer's fantasy of the Diamonds' 1957 doo-wop parody "Little Darlin'," which was so good it turned into the real thing, as this does. "Bop she-waddy, *bop* she-waddy," goes the chorus behind the falsetto lead, which dives down on Kitten as she pushes a stroller on a London street while a construction worker hoots at her, as she invites him "and all the boys" back to her place as his face falls, as she begins to tell the baby in the pram the story of her life—and the movie ends the same way, with Kitten pushing the same stroller, the same baby, which by now we know is the child of her best friend, Charlie, and Charlie's murdered boyfriend, Irwin, the song simultaneously homing in on Kitten like something out of *The Birds* and lifting her feet off the ground. It's the most glorious, irresistible sound imaginable.

Yes, Cillian Murphy's Kitten tells the baby, my mother left me on the doorstep of my father, the local priest, for whom she kept house. Yes, I grew up with a foster family, but when I put on my foster mother's dresses and lipstick, and when I wrote stories in school about my father Father Liam and my mother Eily Bergin and where could I get a sex change, I got in trouble, and I ran away. To join the circus, of course! And then I went to London—

In the circus, or rather with the band Billy Hatchett and the Mohawks, there's Gavin Friday's madman lead singer with his outrageously camped-up version of Johnny Preston's 1960 Indian epic "Running Bear" ("Loved little White Dove," the Big Bopper wrote before stepping onto the plane that would take him, Buddy Holly, and Ritchie Valens to the Happy Hunting Ground), then Kitten onstage as a squaw to Hatchett's chief for Sweet's 1973 "Wig Wam Bam," then Hatchett railing from the stage over "Thirteen dead in Derry" and the evil of British rule and Protestant barbarism in Northern Ireland. There's one of Kitten's favorite songs, Bobby Goldsboro's 1968 "Honey," playing on the radio, entering a scene like weather; there's a generic version of Cole Porter's "Why Am I So Gone (About That Gal?)." As Kitten arrives in London to search for her mother the film offers her Harry Nilsson's 1971 "The Moonbeam Song"; sleeping in doorways, waiting in government offices, wandering the streets with her cardboard suitcase, she's picked up by a man in a car, and it's Bryan Ferry, with sallow, oily skin and a moustache like dirt, who plays Kitten Morris Albert's sallow, oily 1975 "Feelings" on his cassette machine before shoving her head into his lap. She's taken under the wing of a magician ("She came to London, the biggest city in the world," she tells him almost before she tells him her name, "and it swallowed her up"); for his act he hypnotizes Kitten to Dusty Springfield's shimmering 1969 "The Windmills of Your Mind." "I think I see your mother over there," the magician crows, sending Kitten hurtling across nightclub floors to embrace laughing men with the insensate cry of "Mummy!" and then again, "No, over there—" In England to abort the baby she's carrying, Charlie tracks down Kitten and drags her away from the magician, appalled at his cruelty; as they dance in a nightclub, a soldier hits on Kitten. You'll be Bobby, she tells him, as "Honey" plays again; the club is blown up by an IRA bomb and as an Irish survivor, a man disguised as a woman, Kitten is arrested and tortured to the sounds of Buffalo Springfield's 1967 "For What It's Worth." Released, she stares into a store window full of TV sets all playing the theme to the 1955 *Love Is a Many-Splendored Thing*, and the song swallows her as London does. One of the cops who beat her finds her turning tricks on the street, and takes her to the peep show emporium for honest work. A client demands she sing Patti Page's 1953 "How Much Is That Doggie in the Window?"—the one song, it will turn out, that everyone in the film knows, as Kitten and Charlie and eventually Father Liam struggle continually over whether it's "the one with the waggedy tail" or, as the client first screams at Kitten, "'Waggley!'" When Father Liam—played by Liam Neeson, who years before had recorded a version of Van Morrison's spoken-word piece "Coney Island"—appears in her booth, to tell her who her mother is and where she lives, "The Windmills of Your Mind" rises up once more. But it's all prelude.

"I want English," she says as she makes up in her backstage mirror, using Margaret Thatcher's picture in the paper as her model. "I want conservative. I want East Finchley"—Thatcher's constituency. "I want powerful—do you think it works?" She looks hard at herself. "I think I look better than she does," she says. She is about to step out of her picaresque adventures into tragedy, into a real life she has no idea how to make real.

When Van Morrison recorded "Madame George" in 1968, it opened with thirteen seconds of the lightest strum on an acoustic guitar, the quietest fanfare, the most modest and thus the most fatal foreshadowing, as the theme is stated twice: a sense that the story is over before it begins. In the way the film has taken the song into itself, it is over. "Madame George" tells the tale of a Belfast drag queen who with the promise of the forbidden, of drink and cigarettes, drugs and music, sex and fantasy, gathers young boys around herself to stave off a killing burden of loneliness and difference; the song has been placed in the film for those who already know it, for those who will bring the whole of it instantly to bear on who Kitten is and what she is about to do. Its rightness in this moment is so absolute the frisson of the song's appearance creates a kind of swoon. It is so right you can imagine that, at bottom, it is the song that wrote the film, adapted by Neil Jordan and Patrick McCabe from McCabe's novel, which, not having a soundtrack, did not include "Madame George": that the film was made to reach the moment when "Madame George" could play the film rather than the other way around, the song sucking the film into itself, to reveal the pathos of its heroine's quest as nothing else could.

As the first faces come up on the tube-stop escalator, you hear this first body of the song before Kitten's face appears in turn. There is a dream-like synchronicity in the way that Kitten's suit—soft black dots on a white-gray background, black pumps, a small black hat, and strong black vertical stripes on the skirt—matches the silver panels and black borders of the escalator, the panels moving as if of their own will as she, still on the steps, seems pushed by another's hand. Everything moves slowly, inexorably, inevitably.

Like a broom sweeping, a single note from Richard Davis's double bass, the note bending like a finger, beckoning, opens the door of the song—before, the song was poised on the front steps, not ready to enter, not ready to leave. "Down Cyprus Avenue," Morrison sings—but that's not what you hear, and that's not what the scene was made to capture. All the gravity of the moment is in the first word, *down*, itself bent like Davis's first note, into a *dow-nnn*, the tail of the syllable rising; not exactly a word at all, but an exclamation somewhere between a reverie and a curse, a sound that despite the instant it takes to sing or hear contains as much time as you might want to let it echo. The word isn't stretched out but lifted, curled, suspended in the air, something the singer himself can throw out in front of himself and watch.

The song remains on the soundtrack for forty seconds, as Kitten reaches her mother's street and begins to look for her address, the tempo not changing but doubled notes from Davis pressing a single five-line verse in which the listener barely glimpses the figure behind the curtain of the song. As Kitten begins to talk to a pleasant boy of about ten—her half-brother, named Patrick as she was—the music drops down and continues almost silently under the dialogue. The drummer Connie Kay has come in, playing a martial roll with brushes for six seconds, but you can't hear him. Pretending to be an agent for British Telecom, conducting a survey, Kitten begins to ask the boy questions about telephones in his house. "Shouldn't you be asking my mother?" he says.

She's frightened; she's not ready for this, but the boy brings her into his house, and after thirty seconds in the deep background of the film the music lifts sharply up again. From behind, in counterpoint to Kitten's rise on the escalator, we see the back of Kitten's mother's head as she descends the stairs of her house to the foyer, and as you hear Morrison sing "That's when you fall," Kitten sees her mother and crumples to the floor. "That's when you fall," Morrison repeats, but from a distance, as his slightly distorted, echoed voice vanishes into the soundtrack equivalent of a dream dissolve, and as the screen goes black the music goes silent. The match of Morrison's words to the action on the screen would be a cheesy literalism but for the way that, here, the feeling is not that the song is singing the movie, but that the movie is singing the song.

The whole story, the whole quest—Kitten's quest, and Van Morrison's—is in that first word, that single *down*. It's not a studio effect. As Morrison sings certain words, as he finds them, as they find him— "In some ways," he said in 2009, "I'm picking them up from under the surface"—they contain their own echoes, and they echo in other voices. There is Sinéad O'Connor in 1990, twenty-two years after *Astral Weeks* changed the landscape in which she grew up. Now at twenty-four, a year older than Morrison was when he made his album, she is herself crossing from Ireland to London to pronounce, in her soft, thoughtful, steely way, that "England's not the mythical land of Madame George and roses / It's the home of police who kill black boys on mopeds." In the silent places in *Breakfast on Pluto*, Kitten's repeated incantation, "London, the biggest city in the world, and it swallowed her up," combines with the sense of utter devastation and loss that is the engine of "Madame George" to call up Thomas De Quincey in 1803, walking "up and down Oxford-street" with the teenage prostitute Ann, herself then swallowed up by London. In the way that Kitten never reveals herself to her mother, only gazes at her, seated in her mother's living room after her faint and talking about telephones, from two feet away maintaining the distance of her whole life, De Quincey's Ann can hover in the dim shadows of the film, to remind you of how close Kitten comes to refusing her brother's entreaty and walking away, back to her life on the streets of the city, sooner or later turning up dead, never to see her mother, as De Quincey never saw Ann again: "If she lived, doubtless we must have been sometimes in search of each other, at the very same moment, through the mighty labyrinths of London; perhaps even within a few feet of each other—a barrier no wider than a London street, often amounting in the end to a separation for eternity!"

As Morrison sings the first word of "Madame George," all of that can be contained in his *down*, and all of that can be released. It is at the heart of Morrison's presence as a singer that when he lights on certain sounds, certain small moments inside a song—hesitations, silences, shifts in pressure, sudden entrances, slamming doors—can then suggest whole territories, completed stories, indistinct ceremonies, far outside of anything that can be literally traced in the compositions that carry them. Those moments can travel, as the pacing of "Madame George" makes its Cyprus Avenue, a four-block stretch of Belfast, into a thoroughfare as endless as De Quincey's Oxford Street. They can transfer themselves; they can be transferred; they can transfer situations they might inhabit, as "Madame George" briefly inhabits a film about a young Irish transvestite, into realms outside their own literal space—as with, in the long fade of Morrison's *down*, Kitten's rising on the escalator suggests someone rising from the dead, that moment itself rewriting the song, even if Neil Jordan could only afford a little more than a minute of it.

Thomas De Quincy, *Confessions of an English Opium Eater* (1821; New York: Penguin, 1981), 64.

Breakfast on Pluto, dir. Neil Jordan (2005, Sony Pictures Classics). With Cillian Murphy as Kitten, Eva Berthstle as his mother, Eily Bergin, Liam Neeson as Father Liam, Ruth Negga as Charlie, Laurence Kinlan as Irwin, Gavin Friday as

Billy Hatchett, Stephen Rea as Bertle the magician, Bryan Ferry as Mr. Silky String, and Sid Young as Patrick in London.

Rubettes, "Sugar Baby Love" (1974), on *Breakfast on Pluto—Original Soundtrack* (Milan, 2006). Also includes Harry Nilsson's "Me and My Arrow" and "You're Breakin' My Heart," Joe Dolan's "You're Such a Good Looking Woman," Bobby Goldsboro's "Honey," "(How Much Is) That Doggy in the Window?" by Patti Page, "Caravan" by Santo and Johnny, "Feelings" by Morris Albert, "The Windmills of Your Mind" by Dusty Springfield, "Wig Wam Bam" by Gavin Friday, "Sand" by Friday and Cillian Murphy, T-Rex's "Children of the Revolution," and nothing by Van Morrison.

Liam Neeson, "Coney Island," on *No Prima Donna: The Songs of Van Morrison* (Polydor, 1994).

Sinéad O'Connor, "Black Boys on Mopeds," on *I Do Not Want What I Haven't Got* (Capitol, 1990).

THE HEALING GAME. 1997

The black-and-white photo that appears on the face of *The Healing Game*—and on the disc itself, and on the back of the CD box, insisting that you look at it again and again, that you think about it—shows a short, very stocky middle-aged white man on the street, and a taller black man behind him. Both are well-dressed, in dark clothes, with dark hats. The short man, Van Morrison, is wearing blackout glasses and an expensive white shirt buttoned to the neck; the taller man, flugelhorn player Haji Akbar, who wears a white shirt and a striped tie, gazes over Morrison's left shoulder, as if on the lookout for trouble. It is, you can imagine without trying, a mob boss and his number one on their way to settle a score. The expression on Morrison's face, all stone, is appallingly determined and cold.

If this is the mood you carry with you as the music starts, straight away the music tells you you're right: the first lines

of "When That Rough God Goes Riding," the first song, describe "mud-splattered victims . . . all along the ancient
highway," and you catch the echoes of a vendetta as old as
the highway, some internecine tribal conflict that will never
be settled. If as the Sex Pistols rammed it home in 1976 in
"Anarchy in the UK" Morrison's verses call forth the conflict
in Northern Ireland between the UDA and the IRA—and
London's war against Catholic Belfast, the war that began
with Cromwell and continued, as Morrison sang in 1997,
under Tony Blair—the war John Lennon sang about under
Edward Heath, the war Gang of Four sang about under
James Callaghan—the chorus is mythic, outside of any historical time.

As soon as the scene is set everything changes, even if the
story being told holds to its violence. With the first verse
done, Morrison, his voice thick and heavy, glides like an ath-
lete into the chorus, and a tremendous feeling of warmth, of
being in the right place at the right time, takes hold. It carries the listener into a musical home so perfect and complete
he or she might have forgotten that music could call up such
a place, and then populate it with people, acts, wishes, fears.
The deep burr of Morrison's voice buries the words, which
cease to matter; you might not hear them until the tenth
time you play the album, or long after that. "It's when that
rough god goes riding," he sings, drawing the words both
from Yeats and down in his chest, and you might never
know it's the angel of death that has you in its embrace. "I
am this serpent filled with venom," Morrison sings later in
"Waiting Game"—but here his voice, like Vito Corleone's

voice as Robert De Niro plays him, is so filled with quiet, earned authority that you trust it, you ask it to keep speaking to you, to offer you its comfort, even as the man behind it pushes a pillow into your face. The very slowness of the introduction to the song—at first, only piano, the lightest percussion, and Morrison's slurred harmonica, then the way he waits behind syllables even as he voices them—validates everything to follow: validates it musically, emotionally, morally. These first passages create a setting that allows the singer to contemplate the world around himself, and, perhaps for the first time in Morrison's music, to judge it. "I am the god of love and the god of hate," he sings—that is validated. As Morrison all but swallows the words, then lets them shudder in his mouth, it doesn't feel like a grand claim; it feels like what it means to be in the world.

Nearly all of the songs on *The Healing Game* stay on this plane. The melodies build on themselves until they communicate like rhythms; the rhythms, slow and weighted, create a feeling of a definite pace being kept, a pace of readiness. As with Gene Austin's unsettled, visionary 1928 "The Lonesome Road"—filled with specters from the oldest Appalachian ballads, and a backwoods, farmer's kin to "Old Man River," which appeared in the original theatrical production of *Show Boat* the year before*—it's the pace of someone who's seen almost everything, but who knows there might be someone

---

* When the movie version came out in 1929, the producers took no chances: Austin's song was right there too, with Jules Bledsoe's dubbed vocal coming out of Stepin Fetchit's mouth. Morrison recorded a colorless version in 1993.

waiting around the next turn. The volume is never raised. There's no shouting. There's a long walk ahead.

The tunes open up like stories you know in your heart but haven't thought of for years. This is soul music, with the passion of Frankie Laine's "That's My Desire" in 1947, the sadness rolling over a rock 'n' roll beat in Lloyd Price's "Lawdy Miss Clawdy" in 1952, the sympathy of Bobby Bland's "I'll Take Care of You" in 1959, the certainty of Irma Thomas's "Ruler of My Heart" in 1963, the sweep of Aretha Franklin's "Ain't No Way" in 1968, the refusal to walk a step faster or a step slower of Sinéad O'Connor's "Nothing Compares 2 U" in 1990—but without glamour, or even a hint of performance, of gestures extended or notes held for effect. The street this music moves on never disappears.

With "Waiting Game" and the title song, which comes last, *The Healing Game* kept company with Neil Jordan's 1992 film *The Crying Game*, that whole drama of Irish resistance, sexual uncertainty, murderous fate. It was Morrison's best work in more than twenty years. Go back to 1979, for *Into the Music*, a buoyant, serious, playful, blazingly ambitious testament—against *The Healing Game* it sounds thin, poppy, ephemeral, though it isn't remotely so when it's allowed to claim its own air. Morrison's records of the previous seventeen years fade into irrelevance against what he has to offer here. They don't even make sense.

The deep grounding of *The Healing Game* makes me think of the original Fleetwood Mac, the finest flowering of British blues, formed by Peter Green in 1967. As a blues guitarist, Green, who had earlier replaced Eric Clapton in John Mayall's Blues Breakers, had by 1970 been and gone from places—places in the heart, places in the blues—Clapton would never get to. Compared to Them, Fleetwood Mac was a purist band, in quest of the spirit of the Mississippi blues of the 1920s and '30s—though while Them was purist in its own way, in its refusal of the slightest suggestion of levity or even peace of mind, Fleetwood Mac made room for the most raucous rockabilly humor and mercilessly funny parodies of the British blues scene. It was a band of many parts—but while he remained Green was always its center. He played an occult blues, a fantasy blues, where in his most lucid songs and performances—in "Man of the World," "Long Grey Mare," "Albatross," "Trying So Hard to Forget," "Love That Burns," his guitar playing alone on "Something Inside of Me"—every element was slowed down and emotions appeared only to decay.

As a singer, he sang in his own voice. There was never any doubt that he was white and English—and, maybe, little doubt that he was Jewish. The remorse in his voice, you could think, wasn't for the love he'd lost or the life that failed him—the predicament that, sometime around the end of the nineteenth century, the blues was invented to affirm. It was a sorrow over his conviction that as a white Englishman the blues would always be out of his reach. It was that conviction, though, that sense of displacement, that made his blues ring so true: a conviction that in Green's highest moments gave the lie to itself. Over all the years I've listened to his "Love That Burns," trying to keep up with the tragedy it enacts, waiting for the closing guitar part that comes when words have taken the singer as far as they can, but not far enough, forcing him to leave words behind and plead with his bare hands, I don't think I've ever been able to play it twice in a row. It is just too strong.

Morrison came from a similar place, with the same belief in the blues as a kind of curse one puts on oneself, but for a long desert in his career he fled from it, his voice hollowing out along with the placid, reassuring world his music described. Sometimes he fell back before his masters and performed merely as a product of his influences, coming to life the most when he sang with John Lee Hooker; he reached his dead end, with album after album, when he seemed most of all influenced by himself. His music was all self-reference, until solipsism ruled and awarded its crown: the solipsist is always king of his own kingdom, and who willingly gives up a crown? All of that is left behind on *The Healing Game*; as a singer of confidence and pride, Morrison sometimes goes almost as far into the dark as Green did.

Morrison dominates each song on *The Healing Game*— but the word song seems much too small. Like the rough god he sings about, Morrison is astride each incident in the music, each pause in a greater story, but often the most revealing moments—the moments that reveal the shape of a world, a point of view, an argument about life—are at the margins. It might be Pee Wee Ellis's twisting saxophone, or the backing vocals of Katie Kissoon, or the side-singing of Georgie Fame, but each of them brings a certain realism to the setting. Morrison is the philosopher, the man of knowledge and experience; the others are the street he walks on. Ellis's work is too individualistic to rest as mere accompaniment—from the first minutes of *The Healing Game*, his baritone sax and Leo Green's tenor are part of a loose, casual interplay with

Morrison and the other singers, a conversation of asides and pointed fingers. He can make you forget you're listening to a self-evident, self-presenting master, and Morrison, often mumbling, sometimes stepping back from his own lines, as if to question himself, gives Ellis his room. Kissoon and Fame are slight singers, ordinary in every respect; they sing and talk like passers-by, like stand-ins for listeners. In the furious "Burning Ground," which is about getting rid of a body, it's clear who'll be doing the dirty work—Morrison wouldn't give up the pleasure to anyone else. Sounding as gleeful as the Kray Twins—the London gangsters who, with a plan to blackmail Brian Epstein over his homosexuality, supposedly once tried to take over management of the Beatles—Morrison orchestrates the action and gets the kicks. The listener gets to watch.

"I'm not going to fake it, like Johnny Ray," Morrison declaims in the middle of the otherwise unbroken, insistently measured "Sometimes We Cry." It's a cruel dismissal of a once-groundbreaking singer who died miserable and forgotten, just seven years before Morrison put another nail in his coffin—but there's such strength in Morrison's tone it can make you wonder what the cruelty is about.

It was in the early 1950s that Ray, with an emotionalism that was shocking in its nakedness, set the stage for the rock 'n' roll performers, black and white, Bobby Bland no less than Elvis, James Brown no less than David Bowie, who would follow him. "Sometimes We Cry" isn't casually titled—Ray's "Cry" was number one in 1951 for eleven weeks; the flipside, also a huge hit, was "The Little White Cloud That Cried." He was white, frail, with the energy of a dying man reaching out

to grab your neck. "He'd hunch into himself," Nik Cohn
wrote in 1969 in *Pop from the Beginning*,

choke on his words, gasp, stagger, beat his fist against his breast,
squirm, fall forward on to his knees and, finally, burst into tears.
He'd gag, tremble, half strangle himself. He'd pull out every last out-
rageous ham trick in the book and he would be comic, embarrass-
ing, painful, but still it worked because, under the crap, he was in
real agony, he was burning, and it was traumatic to watch him. He'd
spew himself up in front of you and you'd freeze, you'd sweat, you'd
be hurt yourself. You'd want to look away and you couldn't.

Even if it began as a show, the tears coming every night like
Pete Townshend smashing his guitar, soon enough the desperation Ray sparked in his audience blew back at him, and
some nights, in the face of the crowd, he would truly break
down. Then his moment passed. His career collapsed with
arrests in men's rooms and attempts to go straight, both
musically and as a public figure. His obloquy wasn't far
from that of Peter Green, who at the height of Fleetwood
Mac's popularity walked away from the band into religious
insanity, electroshock, institutionalization, years living on
the streets or in the woods, returning finally with his guitar,
his voice, and no spirit, no insight into the music he played,
a once-handsome man covered in fat and matted hair. So
how did Johnny Ray fake it? What was it that he held back?
Was it that, exposed to everyone for who he really was, he
tried to pretend he was just like everybody else—a pathetic
surrender that was itself no less fake than his performance?
Johnny Ray had an act, Morrison seemed to be saying, and

I don't. He tried to pretend that he was just like everybody else; I never have and never will.

In the interstices of *The Healing Game*, in the spaces between the words as Morrison sings them and the notes as he hits them, you can believe it. The depth and mastery of the music Morrison left on that album is such that, for me anyway, it calls up only one real familiar.

Mattie May Thomas was a prisoner at the state penitentiary in Parchman, Mississippi, when on 1 June 1939 the folklorist Herbert Halpert arrived to make recordings. Thomas and other women were gathered in a sewing room. "A made-up song, just about being in prison, alone," Thomas said to introduce what she, or Halpert, titled "Workhouse Blues." Was it made up? All the lines were commonplace, taken from the vast pool of floating verses from which people made their own songs. Thomas began around the time the blues took shape—"In the empty belly, black man, in the year nineteen hundred and nine, I was a little young hobo, all up and down the line"—and then leaped back to the brags, taunts, and japes that were circulating in Davy Crockett's day, a lot of them out of his mouth, or put in it:

> I wrassled with the lions, black man, with the lions on
>   the mountains high
> I pulled they hair out, black man, hair out strand by
>   strand
> Leaping spiders, lord, began to bite my poor heart
> But let me tell you, baby, they crawled away and died
> I wrassled with the hounds, black man, hounds of hell
>   all day

I squeeze them so tight, until they faded away
I swim the blue sea, with the mountains on my back
I mean I conquered all the lions and I even turned they
    power back

Whoever Mattie May Thomas was, she was not a folk singer,
in any meaning of the term.* Coming out of white frontier
settlements, the words were men's words; simply by claiming what is not supposed to be hers, she takes title. That is
the folk process. But the voice is not. It's plainly a profes-
sional voice, a nightclub singer's, "the devil coming out of

---

* Along with "Dangerous Blues," "Big Mac from Macamere," "No Mo'
Freedom," and "Penitentiary Blues" with accompaniment by other
singers, Mattie May Thomas's "Workhouse Blues" first appeared in 1987
on *Mississippi Department of Archives and History Presents Jailhouse Blues:
Women's a cappella songs from the Parchman Penitentiary, Library of Con-
gress field recordings, 1936 and 1939* (Rosetta Records, 1987), with liner
notes by Bernice Johnson Reagon, Leon F. Litwack, Cheri L. Wolfe, and
Rosetta Reitz, with photographs by Dorothea Lange and Marion Post
Walker, including one of the sewing room where the recordings were
made. Minus "Penitentiary Blues," Thomas's recordings gained a wider
audience in 2005 when they were included on the anthology *American
Primitive II—Pre-War Revenants* (Revenant), a collection of recordings by
performers about whom almost nothing was known (according to Reitz,
in her notes to *Jailhouse Blues*, Thomas learned "Workhouse Blues" in a
penal facility in 1926, and served two previous terms at Parchman before
recording there in 1939). A few years later, as entranced by Thomas as I'd
been when I first heard her, it occurred to me that the general release of
 her songs might have sparked someone—a relative, a neighbor,
a friend of a friend—to set down who she was. I googled her—
and there she was, Mattie May Thomas, with her own MySpace
page. An anonymous fan had put it up: her four songs and
someone else's face.

your own mouth":* clear, strong, claiming its own demons, using folkloric words to affirm that the frights and triumphs they describe happened to her and no one else. Like Morrison, Thomas presses words like bricks, then flies over verses toward some unreachable shore of release.

Emotional release, for both, but for Thomas standing for

The fan turned out to be the Greek techno artist who records as Biomass, who later posted videos of his reworkings of Thomas's music. Each takes a Thomas performance and cuts it up, loops it, shuffles words and phrases, repeats them in stuttering echo, adds clicks and hum and whine, and sets it against footage of conflict: a tank speeding through the Iraqi desert; heavily armed police driving back Italian protesters; what might be film from the Vietnam War. Most striking is a piece that opens with split-second flashes of people running separated by much longer segments of black screen. As it goes on, the moments of action imperceptibly lengthen, until you begin to realize you're watching the riots in Paris during May 1968. The glimpses of people and streets accumulate, building a tension to the point of explosion, all to Thomas as if she's looking back on the event, not forward to it, not on some other plane of being, her voice carrying "No mo' freedom" as students throw stones, rush forward, burn cars, are beaten, and even when as a comment on the ameliorating powers of modern capitalism they are replaced by three black women in a nightclub, dressed in furry bikinis and doing the limbo—one of the women giving Thomas the face she now bears.

As I write, you page down to Thomas's 134 MySpace friends, including Nina Simone, Pablo Neruda, Miles Davis, Patti Smith, Sun Ra, Jack Kerouac, Alicia Keys, Janis Joplin, Suicide, James Brown, and Guy Debord, whose 1973 film *La Société du Spectacle* is the clear inspiration for Biomass's "No Mo' Freedom" video. It's something to contemplate: What if these people, almost all of them dead, really had heard Mattie May Thomas? What if those living still haven't? How lucky they are to have that ahead of them.

* A mother's curse on her blues-singing daughter, from Gayl Jones's *Corregidora* (New York: Bantam, 1976).

true release, from prison, and that release symbolizing the shared slaves' dream, shared as fable and prophecy, of flying back to Africa. For Morrison, his own dreams of a Viking's voyage from Denmark to Caledonia and then a magic transport from the old world to the new and back again with ancient songs for a skyway. But if both voices are unique and capable of transcendence, Thomas not at all and Morrison at his fair best never jettison the ordinary, the inescapable, the squalid, the real. For both, it's all in the refusal to be rushed. Ordinary life, after all, guarantees only death and oblivion. Morrison has faced oblivion; though she is almost certainly dead, somehow Mattie May Thomas escaped it, and Morrison may not. In their tone they both say the same thing. Death has waited all these years; it can wait another day.

Nik Cohn, *Awopbopaloobop Alopbamboom*, revised edition of *Pop from the Beginning* (1969; New York: Grove, 1973), 13–14.

"Crime Leaders Kray Twins Schemed to Take Over as the Beatles' Managers," *Entertainment Daily*, 21 June 2009.

Sex Pistols, "Anarchy in the UK" (EMI, 1976).

John Lennon, John & Yoko/Plastic Ono Band, "Sunday Bloody Sunday" and "The Luck of the Irish," on *Some Time in New York City* (Apple, 1972).

Gang of Four, "Armalite Rifle" (Fast, 1978).

Gene Austin, "The Lonesome Road" (1928) collected on *Gene Austin—The Voice of the Southland* (ASV, 1996). Gene Austin's number one hits between 1925 and 1929 included songs that for good or ill have stuck in the American memory: "Yes Sir! That's My Baby," "Five Foot Two, Eyes of Blue," "Forgive Me,"

"My Blue Heaven," "Ramona," and "Carolina Moon." "The
Lonesome Road" reached #10; I have never played it for anyone, over eighty or under twenty, who didn't drift off to another place while listening, or who failed to say "What was
that?" when it was over. Judy Garland and Bobby Darin performed a bright and soulful version on *The Judy Garland Show*,
taped and broadcast just eight days after the assassination of
President Kennedy; see *The Judy Garland Show That Got Away*
(Hip-O DVD, 2002).

Fleetwood Mac, "Albatross," "Long Gray Mare," "Love That
Burns," "Trying So Hard to Forget," (1968), and "Man of the
World" (1969), collected on *The Original Fleetwood Mac—The
Blues Years* (Castle, 1990). Green's work on Fleetwood Mac
member Danny Kirwan's "Something Inside of Me" is best
heard on Fleetwood Mac's *Shrine '69*, a live recording from
Los Angeles (Rykodisc, 1999).

Johnny Ray, *Cry* (Bear Family, 1990). A definitive collection, including "Cry," "The Little White Cloud That Cried" (1951), and Ray's
hit cover of the Prisonaires' "Just Walkin' in the Rain" (1955).

Mattie May Thomas, "Workhouse Blues" (1939), on *American
Primitive Vol. II—Pre-War Revenants (1897–1939)* (Revenant,
2005). Information on Herbert Halpert in Scott Baretta, "The
Parchman Prison Band: From the Cruelest Place on Earth
Came Music," Oxford American #58 (2007).

Biomass, *Market* (Quetempo, Greece, 2006). A CD/DVD that includes both audio and video versions of Mattie May Thomas
performances, though the piece for "Workhouse Blues" is
here all action, no blackout.

Van Morrison, "The Lonesome Road," on *Too Long in Exile*
(Polydor, 1993).

———*The Healing Game* (Polydor, 1997).

PART FOUR

THERE WAS NO FALSE FACE
THE SONG COULD NOT ERASE

INTO THE MUSIC. 1979

It was Morrison's last album before his long swan dive into the pool of contemplation, and it raises a question that all the moments of freedom musicians have contributed to Morrison's own pursuit of freedom—Richard Davis's bass on *Astral Weeks*, Jef Labes's piano on "Linden Arden Stole the Highlights," John Platania's mandolin on "Caledonia Soul Music"—only hint at: is the greatest creative freedom in making a field where others can find it?

This album had Van Morrison's name on it, but it belonged to Toni Marcus, credited on violin, viola, stroviola, and mandolin. Today as Talia Toni Marcus she leads her own jam band; she has fourteen MySpace friends. On *Into the Music*, as it moved out across its fifty minutes, it was an open question whether Morrison was granting freedom to her or if she was granting it to him.

It's a strange album for 1979. Like the old *Oldies But Goodies* albums, it has a "Rockin' Side" and a "Dreamy Side," and one of the songs on the Dreamy Side is a song that actually appeared on the Dreamy Side of an *Oldies But Goodies* album. The first two numbers—"Bright Side of the Road" and "Full Force Gale"—are the most immediately arresting; they fade against what follows. Both have quick rhythms and dashing melodies. On "Bright Side of the Road," near the end, Morrison begins to growl the lines, making himself into a bear, and Marcus swoops over him and then digs into the song. She adds a fervor, a seriousness, that Morrison is dancing away from; he picks up on it, and for a second his words are on the verge of breaking up entirely. Then it's back to a clean wrap-up: you want more.

With "Full Force Gale" everything is tougher from the first beat, and Marcus is on top of the music from the start. It takes Morrison time to catch up with the song—it seems to know things he doesn't. There's a light guitar solo, shadowed by Marcus's violin, and then she picks up the pace and for an instant, before Morrison returns, the tune finds a hardness, again a feeling of conviction, that was missing. But there's a way that even as the beat seems harder and urgency greater, the song drags against itself. It's a void in the music that took over entirely when in 1996 Morrison re-recorded the song as if its message were being delivered by a procession of defeated—or not very interested—old men shuffling down the street in heavy overcoats: "Like a full force gale. I was lifted up again. I was lifted up again. By the Lord."

The Rockin' Side is really rocking with "Stepping Out Queen." It's pleasant enough as Morrison sings it, but even he seems to know how it will double in size when he turns it over to Marcus; it's there in the sense of announcement when he simply says, "Alright." The word carries a colon: what opens up is a labyrinth, and within seconds you can't find your feet. You can't tell where the music's coming from, whether it's one piece or four, whether it's a human being playing or a Hindu god with eight hands. Marcus's violin dives for the song, and her viola counters the rush with an elegance you want to pause with. The violin presses its demands, but all along there's been a screech in the background, and now as it rises little notes like birds flutter around it, to cage it, failing as the sound goes into the territory first broken by John Cale's viola in "Heroin"— which now is also the sound of a woman getting dressed.

Here it's clearly Morrison opening the doors of his songs to another musician, giving her the spotlight until he has to take it back. But on the Dreamy Side that changes.

"And the Healing Has Begun" is one of Morrison's signature songs—but at its heart it is his, a book of desires he can embrace without shame, because he has passed it on to someone else. It begins with confidence, a lack of fear. With a bend toward the past that would turn up such riches nearly thirty years later with "Behind the Ritual," the singer promises that he and the woman he's singing to will go back to the avenue they once knew and that once knew them. They'll get out those *Oldies But Goodies* albums; they'll "sing a song from way back when." This is a man walking down the street with wings on his feet, who can't wait, who's consumed by the vision in front of him: her red dress. She's got to wear it. But then for a long passage the song all but breaks off, and for what seems like minutes Toni Marcus allows Morrison to do almost nothing, to get lost in his own song, to wander away from it, certain it will be there when he gets back. For chorus after chorus she's the first voice of the song, pushing it with her violin into a realm of pure freedom, where anything can be said but nothing needs to be. "Alright," Morrison says. "Yeah." "Whoo"—and Marcus presses on, all but sawing her arm off. Morrison comes back stronger, inspired, ready to reclaim the song. "That backstreet rock 'n' roll," he says, "that's where it comes from, man," with *it* morally enormous, everything he or you might ever care about—and the honesty in the way he says it is overwhelming, a truth he finally feels free to let loose in the air. Marcus is merely accompaniment. Then she seems captured by the song, and she shoots out ahead of the singer, and he calls a halt. "Wait a minute, baby—listen, listen, listen, listen"—and he's not talking to her, and he's not talking to the woman who's going to put on the red dress.

There's a woman on the street. He stops her. He starts chatting her up, inveigling himself into her apartment. It's "Gloria" in reverse, and with the insistence of that opening "Gloria" riff—someone running down the street and banging on every door he passes—replaced by a man talking, hesitating, and less to seduce her than to seduce himself. For everything has to be exactly right: she has to move behind the door. "Ah, move on up this, ah, letter box here." He wants to play a Muddy Waters record he's found in her apartment. "Come on in for some of this backstreet jelly roll," he says, as if bowing back to Muddy, and with that the woman disappears. His tone is all low vowels, as if he's talking to himself, as if this is all happening in his head. Marcus has been there all along, simply repeating the theme of the song, and when Morrison again rises up with a celebratory chant, the first woman back again in her red dress, it's the one-night stand back there in the song that stays.

Merely as a story, "It's All in the Game" is in the all-time top ten. It began as a violin piece by one John G. Dawes, born in 1865 in Ohio, a financier and amateur musician who one day in 1911 stumbled on what he called "Melody in A Major": "It's just a tune that I got in my head, so I set it down." A friend got it published; it stayed alive, even as Dawes went on to a career as a civic activist, forming an alliance to fight the growing influence of the Ku Klux Klan in Ohio, Michigan, and the Midwest, in 1925 sharing the Nobel Peace Prize for helping to revive the German economy after the First World War, then serving as vice president of the United States under Calvin Coolidge from 1925 to 1929.

In 1951 a journeyman songwriter named Carl Sigman decided to take a crack at what he knew as "The Dawes Melody"; with words, with a narrower range, he heard a hit. Working with Mac Goldman of Warner Bros. Music, which owned Dawes's composition, Sigman brought in his word sheet the day Dawes died. "Your lyric must have killed him," Goldman said.

> Many a tear has to fall
> But it's all
> In the game
> All in the wonderful game
> That we know
> As love

You have words
With him
And you future's
Looking dim
But these things
You heart can rise
Above

Once in a while he won't call
But it's all
In the game
Soon he'll be there at your side
With a sweet
Bouquet
And he'll kiss
Your lips
And caress your waiting fingertips
And your hearts
Will fly
Away*

The song went first to Tommy Edwards, a nightclub crooner. His recording went to #18—an almost meaningless success. In those days very few records were released with a chance at certified national popularity—most country or rhythm and blues records were excluded in advance. Almost anything

---

* Sigman also wrote a spoken introduction: "Remember this: Where love's concerned, at times you'll think your world has overturned. But if he's yours, and you're his, remember this—"

backed by a major label—Edwards was on RCA—made the top twenty, at least for a week, after which it would be covered by a dozen other people. In those days, there weren't that many songs respectable enough for the likes of Dinah Shore, or even Louis Armstrong, both of whom immediately cut their own "It's All in the Game." Edwards's version was paltry: waltz time, Rimsky-Korzakov strings that seem to come from another room, they have so little to do with the song. Edwards seems to be rehearsing—there's that much heart in his delivery. Within his smooth tone, he doesn't seem to know or care what the song might say, and it dies a third of the way in.

By 1958, Edwards was on the skids. Rock 'n' roll had put his career in the toilet. Singers like Fats Domino and Little Richard and Chuck Berry and a nation's worth of other people who couldn't fit into Edwards's tuxedo and wouldn't deign to were writing their own songs and they owned the charts. So he gave in. He redid "It's All in the Game" with a doo-wop arrangement: a doo-wop backing chorus, more importantly strolling doo-wop piano triplets, a light guitar, strings buried. But it was the vocal that this time made "It's All in the Game" Carl Sigman's biggest hit, Tommy Edwards's biggest hit, a huge number one hit, and in the twists of American history, the one reason John G. Dawes is still spoken of: you argue, he turns his back, you wait, once in a while he won't call, but it's all in the game, that wonderful game we call love, and then he's back, with a smile, flowers, in Sigman's best and most unlikely line, "to caress your waiting fingertips"—and Edwards offers the tale in sadness, regret, as if he's been through this many times and it's too late for him but he's going to pass on what knowledge he's gleaned to you.

It became a standard, done over the years by Bobby Bland, Jackie DeShannon, Elton John—and in 1964, in England, by Cliff Richard. When Van Morrison takes it up, he's right back in the middle of "And the Healing Has Begun." It's barely a performance; it seems to resist taking any shape at all.

"Uhhh—yeah—*yeah*"—he's feeling his way around the song. "Alright." "Whoo. Yeah." He's arguing with the lyric, looking for something that moves him—and "Your future's looking dim," the song's cheapest line, doesn't. But then he finds a place for himself: "Once in a while he won't call—but I heard you." He breaks the song down, into spaces where he can touch what the man in the song is touching: "Just like that." But when Morrison says, "And your heart will—*yeah*—fly away," the last two words are so small, like fireflies, that in their lightness the song takes on an emotional weight it's never had before, in all of its long life. And there's a seductive curl he puts on those two words. The yarragh was just a sound back on that first number, in the growls of "Bright Side of the Road," but now, with Morrison deepening the old song, it's a whisper, and a spell. As with everyone who came before him, Morrison is the witness, the guide, the narrator, but like nobody else he steps into the song as its ghost lover.

Tommy Edwards, "It's All in the Game" (RCA Victor, 1951, 1958).
1958 version included on *Oldies But Goodies, Vol. 7* (Original

Sound, 1963), along with (Rockin' Side) "Tequila" by the Champs, "New Orleans" by Gary (U.S.) Bonds, "Runaround Sue" by Dion, "I Know" by Barbara George, "Handy Man" by Jimmy Jones, "Bumble Boogie" by B. Bumble and the Stingers, and (Dreamy Side) "I Love How You Love Me" by the Paris Sisters, "Donna" by Ritchie Valens, "Teen Angel" by Mark Dinning, the Chimes' "Once in a While," and Jerry Butler's "He Will Break Your Heart." The 1951 version is not included on any Tommy Edwards collections but can be found on YouTube; see below.

Carl Sigman Songs (MajorSongs, 2003). Produced by the unmatchable Gregg Geller, a three-disc collection of recordings of Sigman's compositions, including numbers by, among many others, Count Basie with Helen Humes, Benny Goodman with Helen Forrest, Mildred Bailey, Louis Armstrong, Billie Holiday, Louis Prima, Frank Sinatra (including "Ebb Tide"), Dean Martin, Ella Fitzgerald, the Angels, Cilla Black, Shirley Bassey, Peggy Lee ("Shangri La"), Aretha Franklin, Esther Phillips, Ben E. King, the Righteous Brothers ("Ebb Tide" again, and a hit again), Sonny and Cher, Darlene Love ("It's a Marshmallow World," produced by Phil Spector for the 1963 *A Christmas Gift for You*), Tom Jones, Sarah Vaughan, Jerry Lee Lewis, Joni Mitchell, and the Specials, with "It's All in the Game" by Tommy Edwards (both versions), Morrison, the Four Tops, and Merle Haggard.

Van Morrison, "Full Force Gale" (1996), included on *Catalog Strays 1965–2000* (Wild Card bootleg).

———*Into the Music* (Warner Bros., 1979).

FRIDAY'S CHILD. 1971

In 1994, for a Van Morrison tribute album that Morrison himself co-produced, the fine British soul singer Lisa Stansfield took up "Friday's Child," a song Morrison cut with Them in its last days, a recording that went unreleased at the time. It was a brave choice; the song defeated her. She hit all the right notes and made none of them stick. Backing singers repeated Stansfield's "Don't stop" in staccato, "Don't! Stop!" as if for emphasis, but all they did was stop the music; when they repeated "Friday's child, Friday's child," their plug-in tone made whatever Stansfield had done that seemed real feel fake. The soul tricks Stansfield used—pauses meant to spark a sense of suspense that collapsed instantly into melodrama, moans, high murmurs to herself, as if to indicate an emotion too rich to communicate directly—came across as tricks. Nevertheless, there was something instructive, even interesting, about what Stansfield had done with the song:

you could catch the words. "Monday's child is fair of face / Tuesday's child is full of grace / Wednesday's child is full of woe / Thursday's child has far to go / Friday's child is loving and giving"—in this song, heedlessly. Stansfield told the song's story: a cautionary tale for someone who burns up the ground behind himself or herself, sleeps with anyone who gives them the eye, stays up all night drinking and doping, and trusts everyone who takes everything he can steal.

When Morrison sang it the song was its own wind; as its own wind it blew its own words away. With Them, Morrison was tentative; still, after a verse, the wind began to rise, and a passion far too great for any words to contain was on the horizon. It never got any closer, but it made you lean toward it emotionally, wanting to know what it knew, even if the words "You got something, they all want to know" ("You got something, they don't want to know," in Stansfield's one fascinating moment) had already gone right past you. "You can't stop now," Morrison sang in 1966, for the first time unfurling a flag he would wave for years to come at the end of his shows, but it had nothing to fight against.

At Pacific High Studios in San Francisco five years later a performance is about to erupt that will make "Just Like a Woman" into a warm-up, even if, this night, "Friday's Child" came first. There's a fanfare on the piano, then a military drum roll before Morrison takes hold of the song. Because the song is yet to really begin you do hear the first words, but they are so big for a beginning, so full of a quest that could be taking place at any time and could go anywhere, the words sung with such fervor that a whole, huge

map of the world might appear before you as you hear
them—

> From the north
> To the south
> You walked all the way

—the words don't necessarily register. The verse proceeds,
still nothing but piano and drums, but as if they've doubled
themselves, the pressure increasing, the warning the song
was written to be emerging in the shape of its own body, so
that when a guitarist begins to count toward the looming
chorus, and then backing singers dig down deep for what it
will take to match Morrison's own leaping incantations,
they seem to have been there all along. What happens now,
as a trombone plays off the bass drum to make a single instrument, a single crumbling wall, is frightening—this is a
warning so strong it has rushed right by its subject, that person who was all so ready for the world he or she walked all
the way, to take on the world as such. And you know you're
in for it.

In *Control*, Anton Corbijn's 2007 film about the late-
1970s Manchester band Joy Division, the four young men
take the stage for the first time, the actors themselves playing
and singing—and when they finished "Transmission" I realized half a minute had gone by and I hadn't taken a breath.
What Sam Reilly as the singer Ian Curtis had done with his
face even more than his voice was as shocking as anything I'd
ever seen on a screen.

That's what happens here. The out-of-nowhere assaults in "Just Like a Woman," those split-second explosions of rancor and desire, will here be the whole song.

The ensemble drops back, again leaving only the piano player and the drummer, but its arrival was so thrilling it remains as a shadow, a threat that could return at any time. A saxophonist has begun to noodle behind Morrison, like someone wandering in from another room, too stoned to notice he's barged into someone else's song. "You got," Morrison shouts, his volume high, a sense of abandon pushing against his control of every word, the tension between abandon and control turning each word into a bomb, with the feeling that the singer is himself frightened by his own words, "to hold on,"

> Hold
> Hold
> Hold
> Hold
> Hold
> Hold
> Hold it—

The second chorus clamps down, the desperation in the title phrase so intense you can't imagine where it is that's left to go. Everyone pulls back—and inexplicably, as if maybe each and every one of them has gone as far as they can (maybe everyone needs a drink, needs a cigarette), they leave the song to the saxophonist.

It might be the worst instrumental break in the history of the form. Meandering, tripping over his own feet, bumping into the amplifiers, hitting sour notes again and again, the saxophonist takes you out of the song, out of the music, out of the building, into the street, and not up to your room with Gloria following to knock on your door as soon as you've closed it, merely back to your car, which has a smashed right window and a ticket on the windscreen.

But a certain gravity has already made itself felt; you can't see it, you can't necessarily feel it even if you try to call it back, but as soon as the band returns it's as if it never left. They begin right where they left off, at the edge of the same cliff; if anything they're closer to the edge. As Morrison presses on, the guitarist begins to chime, quietly, tiny high notes building toward a finale that is already present as an inevitability, a presence that already gainsays whatever might be left to be said.

The chiming gets louder. Morrison begins to pound single words, one sequence after another. "Even even even even even" shoots out like white water, but "Watch it! Watch it! Watch it!" pulls against the momentum of the band—it couldn't be more sudden or complete if Morrison were holding up the flat of his hand. In the drama in which Morrison has trapped you, at first it might seem that he's doing this to forestall the fate of the person to whom the song is addressed: to save her, to save him. But as soon as that thought appears, if it does, it turns on itself. What you're hearing is the singer's rage that it's too late, his bitterness that no one listened, no one heard, that it didn't have to end this way.

They reach the chorus again. It goes on, doubled, tripled, "You can't stop, you can't stop, you can't stop now," the backing singers turning a somersault, "Can't stop now, can't stop now, Friday's child," for a full minute and a half, and it's transporting, but it doesn't matter. The song had already ended, back there in the middle of the curse, the singer pleading with his charge to hold on to what she or he had, knowing he or she had already given it away.

There's applause. Morrison goes right into "Que Sera, Sera"—"I asked my mother, what shall I be"—which turns out to be an introduction to "Hound Dog."

Control, dir. Anton Corbijn (2007; Genius DVD, 2008).

Lisa Stansfield, "Friday's Child," on *No Prima Donna: The Songs of Van Morrison* (Polydor, 1994).

Them, "Friday's Child," collected on *The Story of Them Featuring Van Morrison* (Polydor, 1998).

Van Morrison, "Friday's Child," on *The Inner Mystic: Recorded Live at Pacific High Studios, California, Sept. 1971* (Oh Boy/Odyssey bootleg of complete Pacific High Studios concert, as broadcast 1971 on KSAN-FM, San Francisco).

MADAME GEORGE. 1968

"With a record as evocative as *Astral Weeks*," Josh Gleason said to Van Morrison in 2009, for a high-profile NPR piece on the occasion of the release of *Astral Weeks Live at the Hollywood Bowl*, "there's a nagging desire to understand what in your life inspired it—to know where the songs come from, what they mean."

"No, no, no, because, it's not *about* me," Morrison said with a vehemence that didn't sound defensive—as his denials, of anything, so often do. "It's totally fictional. These are *short stories*, in musical form—put together of composites, of conversations I heard, things I saw, and movies, newspapers, books, and *comes out* as stories. That's it," he said, though already his tone had shifted to that of utter wonder that people won't accept this. "There's no more."

It wasn't the first time he'd had to answer the question, which he'd never done in a manner anyone liked. "Did you have anyone in particular in mind?" the folk singer Happy Traum asked Morrison in 1970; it was Morrison's first *Rolling Stone* interview. "Did you know anyone like that?" "Like what?" Morrison said, his guard up in an instant. "What's Madame George look like? What are you trying to say . . . in front. So I know." "It seems to me to be the story of a drag queen," Traum said reasonably. "Oh no," Morrison said. "Whatever gave you that impression? It all depends on what you want, that's all, how you want to go. If you see it as a male or a female or whatever, it's your trip. How do I see it? I see it as a . . . a Swiss cheese sandwich." "Everybody gives me a quizzical look, a question mark stare, and they think I know what they're talking about," Morrison said after a moment, stepping back, trying to explain. "'What about like blah blah blah . . . ' and they expect me to go 'Yeah!' It's just not that simple."

Eight years later he was again talking to *Rolling Stone*, this time with Jonathan Cott, whose technique as an interviewer has always been to elicit the most direct responses by throwing out the most off-the-wall questions, usually asking his subjects if they agreed with the sentiments expressed by, say, the Hasidic rabbi Dov Baer, "the Mazid of Mezeritch." In this instance Cott stayed closer to home: "A friend of mine thinks Madame George is a perfume—you sing the name as 'Madame Joy,' and then there's that scent of Shalimar." "It seems to me to be the story of a drag queen," Morrison said, as if he were Happy Traum and Cott were Morrison, except that he was laughing, and despite the fact that he had already told someone else that Cott's friend might as well claim the prize: "The original title was 'Madame Joy' but the way I wrote it down was 'Madame George.' Don't ask me why I do this because I just don't know." "The question is," Cott went on, missing a step, "who's singing the song?" "The question might really be," Morrison said, in a friendly manner, but with a gesture toward another plane of meaning that could not have been more pronounced if he'd knocked the writer's notepad out of his hand, "is the song singing you?"

This was nearly three decades before the one-time rock critic Tom Nolan—perhaps following Morrison's suggestion to his biographer John Collis that "Madame George" might have had something to do with his great-aunt Joy, who he, Morrison, thought might have been clairvoyant—argued for the *Wall Street Journal* that Madame George was in truth George "Georgie" Hyde-Lees, the wife of William Butler Yeats, known conventionally as Madame George Yeats, who died in 1968, the year "Madame George" appeared. She was a spiritualist who sparked Yeats's work with automatic writing dictated by the dead, a technique Morrison, who in 1984 recorded Yeats's "Crazy Jane on God" in a cracked voice, has used when blocked, cutting up copies of *People* magazine, rearranging parts of headlines and text, divining a line for a song . . . and never mind that the given name of both Van Morrison and his father is George. If the character cannot be permitted to be made up, if it must be real—to borrow a phrase from another Irishman, well, as well her as another.

The tyranny of tying anything an artist might do or say to his or her own life, to give it the weight of the real, and switch off the lights on the weightlessness of the imagination—a philistine fear of art that found its most spectacular form in the JT Leroy hoax, which only seemed to convince people

that while taking fiction for autobiography remained the
highest form of understanding, it was worth making sure that
the person whose autobiography one was plumbing actually
existed—was summed up all too well by John Irving in 1979.
We were talking about the scene in *The World According to
Garp* where Garp's son Walt is killed, and about the many
readers who'd written to him, saying, "I lost a child, too"—
believing that any story that hit them so hard had to be true.
"How do you respond to those letters?" I asked him. "Do you
have any answer to those letters?" "I always answer those letters," he said. "Those are the serious ones; those are the ones
that matter."

I have had two or three friends who went through that, and their reactions were very matterful to me—and I guess the letters that I really felt
drawn to respond to were those from people who, in that old way,
again, would write me one letter, *assuming* that this had to be my experience, too. And when I would write back—sort of a condolence and a
thank-you for responding to the book—I felt I had to *say*, no, this is
not my misfortune. Then I developed a number of ways of saying, well,
it's enough to have had children to imagine what it would be like to
lose them. But this, of course, assumes an imagination of immense
paranoia on the part of everyone, which everyone may not have.

I found people writing back to me a second time, some of them
unable to conceal their resentment: they felt tricked. They felt they
had been *taken in* by the book. They came to the book with open
arms, saying this is genuine, this is true, that hurt in all the real
ways—and then to find out that it was only imagined—

I *live* by my imagination, and yet even I can be influenced by how
the imagination is mistrusted by the rest of the world, by the way

fiction is discredited by *non*-fiction. I've been on airplanes and people say, "Hi, Ken, Kansas City, what do you do?" I say, "Oh, I write." "Oh, what do you write?" "Novels." "Oh, ah, *fiction* . . . " Immediately: you know what I mean! It's just this *shitting on from the word go.*

In Mary Gaitskill's novel *Two Girls Fat and Thin*, a writer takes up the challenge of imagining whole worlds out of glimpses, out of a walk down the street:

The evening was cool and vague. Justine watched everyone who walked past her, and irksome tiny acts about them entered her orbit and clustered about her head. A young couple approached her, the man with his square pink head raised as if he were looking over a horizon, his hands thrust angrily in his pockets, his slightly turned-out feet hitting the ground with dismal solidity, his cheap jacket open to his cheap shirt. The woman on his arm crouched into him slightly, her artificially curled hair bounded around her prematurely lined face, her pink mouth said, "Because it's dishonest to me and to everybody and even yourself." Justine looked headlong into the open maw of their lives; they passed, and the pit closed up again.

It doesn't matter if Gaitskill actually walked down a street where someone said the words that in her paragraph appear in quotation marks. A moment this closely observed has already gone beyond the limits of observation; it is already imagined. That is why any talk of the real, the lived, the experienced as a legitimation or validation of aesthetic response—really, nothing more than a permission for us to be moved by what we are in fact moved by—is a red herring at best. There are only two reasons people try to track Madame George down, to link her to a real person: because the character is itself powerful, full of allure, and because of our own fear of the imagination, our fear that we are vulnerable to some trifle somebody else merely thought up. But Morrison's translation is better: are you letting the song sing you, or are you trying to sing the song?

So let your imagination open up and drift. Let Madame George tell you who she is. Who do you think of? I think of Michael Jackson. I think of Marianne Faithfull, telling the same sixties stories—the sixties as the New Jerusalem, and she its consort, mother, and Merlin—over and over again, always with a glamour that is both grimy from use and full of its own imperious light, qualities you can hear in Faithfull's own recording of "Madame George." I think of the mother of one of my eighth-grade classmates. With her daughter as a front, she would hold parties for the class, fifteen of us from a Quaker school on the San Francisco Peninsula. She was the first bohemian I ever encountered: a single mother, when that was strange, if not a scandal, who dressed in silk, in long, loose dresses. She was heavily made up. While she never gave us alcohol, it was all around, fancy bottles displayed on tables and in cabinets, like a hint of future pleasures, and she always seemed drunk. She showed us her gun. She seemed to need to be around young people. At thirteen in 1958 this was seductive—and a relief to leave behind, to move on to high school, where, a few years later, one or two of my new classmates found their way to Ken Kesey's acid farm, just up the road in La Honda, as she might have also, unless she faded away, chasing her own daughter's youth until it too was used up.

Morrison first recorded "Madame George" for Bert Berns's Bang label in November 1967, as *Blowin' Your Mind!* was climbing its way to #182 on the charts—a version not released until long after Berns's death, and until long after the song, as it appeared on *Astral Weeks*, had achieved the kind of hermetic glow that transcends fame. Here it's a production, as if at a party or a nightclub, with dead-end ambiance. Morrison is sarcastic, even sneering; behind him the Sweet Emotions do "the colored girls go" exactly as Lou Reed always heard it. The people in the audience, if this is a club, or on the couches and in the kitchen or in the doorways if it's an apartment, are distracted, ignoring the singer, everyone talking and drinking. There's bass, tambourine, and an electric guitar playing stripper blues like something out of the roadhouse scene in *Twin Peaks: Fire Walk with Me*, where women wander through the crowd naked and the floor is covered with a layer of cigarette butts that except for the dancers' feet hasn't been disturbed since the place opened. Morrison fights for space, draping cool over himself like an overcoat. It's as if he needs to satirize the material to protect himself from it—or to protect the song from the crowd, which is to say the producer. "Then your self-control lets go / Suddenly you're up against the bathroom door," he says in lines that would be gone by the time he sat down with Connie Kay, Richard Davis, Lewis Merenstein. The crowd is egging him on, then yelling and shrieking. The music is busy and burdened. "We know you're pretty far out," Morrison says, as if his stand-up act is just about to completely dry up, as if all he's really doing is schmoozing music business hustlers, as if he'd rather be anywhere else. "I've got a tape in Belfast with all my songs on that record"—from *Blowin' Your Mind!*—"done the way they're supposed to be done," he said after a show in early 1969, at the Avalon Ballroom in San Francisco. That night his own acoustic guitar completed a combo of a stand-up bassist and the *Astral Weeks* hornman John Payne; Morrison sang every song from *Astral Weeks* along with "Who Drove the Red Sports Car" and "He Ain't Give You None" from *Blowin' Your Mind!* which now took on drifting, *Astral Weeks* rhythms. "It's good and simple, it doesn't come on heavy. 'T. B. Sheets' isn't heavy, it's just quiet. It was the producer who did it, and the record company. They had to cover it with the big electric guitar and the drums and the rest. It came out wrong and they released it without my consent."

Morrison and Berns had been fighting over the record, and everything else—*Blowin' Your Mind!* advances eaten up by expenses, royalties deferred against returns, management contracts, publishing contracts, production contracts—when Berns dropped dead of a heart attack at the end of 1967. There were people who thought Morrison had yelled him to death. There were threats from people who knew how to make good on them,* and there was the demand from Berns's widow that Morrison produce the thirty-six new

---

* A photo taken at a Bang Records launch party for Morrison—a launch party held on a boat—shows a tipsy Morrison, a beaming Janet Planet, the Brill Building songwriter and Berns associate Jeff Barry, Berns himself as a ringer for Gene Vincent, and a big man with a bigger cigar sticking out of his mouth like a screwdriver—the most mobbed-up-looking picture of the New York record business I've ever seen.

songs he had owed Berns's publishing company, and that he
now owed her.

Thus one day in 1968, not long before he began recording
Astral Weeks, in order to escape his contracts with Berns and
retrieve the freedom to record again on his own terms,* Morrison sat down with his guitar and Lewis Merenstein and
taped thirty-one numbers, seemingly in approximately the
thirty-five minutes it takes to play them: "Twist and Shake,"
"Shake and Roll," "Stomp and Scream," "Scream and Holler,"
and "Jump and Thump," five variations on Berns's Isley
Brothers hit "Twist and Shout"; "Hang On Groovy," a flip of
the bird to Berns's hit "Hang On Sloopy" with the McCoys;
the likes of "Just Ball," "Ringworm," "Blow in Your Nose,"
"Nose in Your Blow," "You Say France and I Whistle," "I Want
a Danish," and "The Big Royalty Check." But there are two
performances that don't parody themselves. One is "Goodbye
George," if only for the stately "Like a Rolling Stone" chords
that open it. "Goodbye, George," Morrison sings soulfully.
"Here comes—" The song seems about to turn into a farewell
to Berns himself—until "Here comes" is followed not by "the
night" but "number forty-five, in Argentina."

But with the next cut, "Dum Dum George," the melody
of "Madame George" as it would emerge on *Astral Weeks* is
instantly and completely in place. This and the real song
begin in the same mood, with the same count—even if

---

* While agreeing to include two Berns estate–owned compositions,
which turned out to be "Madame George" and "Beside You," a version
of which Morrison had also recorded with Berns, on any new album.

Morrison is dismissing Lewis Merenstein's entreaties before either had the chance to make anything more of them than this. "This is the story of Dum Dum George," Morrison says as the theme continues. "Who came up to Boston, one sunny afternoon"—and there is that "Madame George" minor-key drop. "He drove up from New York City . . . and he was freaky. And he wanted to record me. And I said, 'George, you're dumb.' And he said, 'I know. Why do you think I make so much money? I want to do . . . a record . . . that'll make number one.' Dumb dumb." Ilene Berns listened to the tape and let the other five compositions Morrison owed her slide.

It's spooky to hear the song find its voice ahead of the moment when that voice would take shape. "That's what we got on tape," Morrison said in 2009 of the *Astral Weeks* sessions that followed. "Another performance might have been totally different. That was that performance, on those days." That sense of accident and serendipity takes over. "Madame George" as one can hear it today sounds most of all unlikely, not something that could be traced to anything in the singer's immediate circumstances, his past, his idols (though Lead Belly's "Alabama Bound" is here too, as it is all over Morrison's music). The possibility that the throwaway one minute and twenty-seven seconds of "Madame George" that Morrison recorded before encountering musicians with whom he would make *Astral Weeks* might be all there was hits home in the same way that one might worry that the day would come when one would put on "Madame George"—or any song one thought was as rich as life itself—and it would turn up dead.

For me there is always a sense of worry when I put the album on again. Will it sound as true, will it sound as good as before, will there come a time when I will be listening to the end of "Madame George" and suddenly it's already there, I've heard it, it has nothing left to tell me—and that has never happened. It has never worn out. It's never given itself up.

Is that because it has no ending? When I think idly about *Astral Weeks*, walking down the street, something in the air or in the carriage of the person next to me reminding me of a turn of phrase or a pause somewhere on the album, it doesn't end with "Slim Slow Slider," the last song of the eight that comprise it. It ends with "Madame George," which is only the fifth song—and that is because of what happens after Richard Davis hits that note that, for him, has said all the song had left to say.

The scene has been set, and all the players have wandered into it. In George's apartment, with the frayed damask cushions and the heavy drapes making the air close, the boys watch as George changes the LPs and 78s on the box, handling each so carefully, thumbs never touching the grooves, strange records by Billie Holiday and Charlie Parker that speak a different language, they watch as George turns her Ouija board, they watch her smoke, they watch when in panic she thinks the police are near and rushes to throw her dope out the window—"down into the street below." Even when the boys are doing all these things themselves—playing with the Ouija board, speaking the secret jazz language, which in this place is their language, the language they speak to each other as if "Kokomo" or "I Cover the Waterfront" are clues to real life and a code to keep the square world at bay, smoking dope, gathering it up to toss it away—they feel as if they're watching.

There is the long section when all the boys turn their back on her and walk away—into adulthood, responsibility, idleness, dope-dealing, addiction, wealth, respectability, renown, and, never, what she already represents, with the makeup caking on her eyes, the sweat rotting the foundation, the wig slipping, her speech slurring, the laughter too loud, the need in the way she waves you goodbye ("Hey love, you forgot your glove") too obvious: death. The singer has to get all the way away, taking a train out of the city, maybe even leaving the country, the pennies he throws out of the window onto the bridges below at once a way of pretending he's still a little boy and an echo of George's dope falling to the street, all one long fall. Here are the great passages of repetition, where you cannot imagine the song can end. *Dry your eye dry your eye dry your eye dry your eye dry your eye dry your eye dry your eye* and on thirteen times, more, as if it's all been a breath being drawn, a pause to launch the more bitter, withdrawing, fleeing *And the love that loves the love that loves the love that loves the love that loves to love the love that loves to love the love that loves the glove*, all with the burr of a trumpet coming down like an execution, the blade of the guillotine raised and dropped again and again long after the head has been passed from hand to hand in the crowd. And this is only prelude to what Morrison will do with the word "goodbye," what he will do murmuring, singing ooos and woos as if he's found them on the copy of "Earth Angel" that one day a DJ forgot to take off the turntable, a record that played on after the DJ

was fired and after the station shut down, a signal in the
ether sustained by its own power.

One day in 2000 I walked into the Portland Art Museum
to find the Dick Slessig (as in dyslexic) Combo—Carl Bronson, bass, Mark Lightcap, guitar, Steve Goodfriend, drums—
half an hour into a performance of what would turn into
ninety minutes before I realized that the nearly abstract,
circular pattern they were offering as the meaning of life—
it was all they were playing, anyway—was from George Mc-
Crae's 1974 Miami disco hit "Rock Your Baby." Or rather the
pattern wasn't from the tune, it was the tune, the thing itself.
Variation was never McCrae's point (the big moment in
"Rock Your Baby," the equivalent of the guitar solo, is when
he barely whispers "Come on"); finding the perfect, self-
renewing riff was. "I could listen to that forever," I said to
Bronson when he and the others finally stepped down for a
break. "We'd play it forever if we were physically capable,"
he said.

They were also playing "Madame George." When Morrison dives into the words, the syllables, that will seem to divest him of flesh, leaving only a word, the word repeating
until it has remade a body of flesh to hold it, until it can
walk like a man, the feeling is that the singer has lived this
out many times before, the word always evading him, until
the day when it happened that certain people came together in the right place at the right time and the body was,
for the ten minutes it took to play the song, found.

The ending, as it begins again with Davis's moral exit, is
so long, so drawn out, so dramatic and scary, I get chills
thinking about it, let alone listening to it. As the train pulls

off, it seems a whole body of memory is dropping away, has been cut off to drift away on the sea. In the trick your mind plays on you, the drama "Madame George" enacts might be the end of the record because nothing could follow it. That's the end of the story—and yet because of the way that ending is so drawn out, each repeating word or syllable doubling back on itself, the song doesn't ever really end, and in fact the ending is false. As you listen you hear that no one present, not the singer, the producer, the musicians, not even Richard Davis can actually make the song stop, and so as you listen, and reach the end, and there is a pause before the next song, "Madame George" seems to be still playing. When you merely let the song play in your mind, catching perhaps for the first time that at the very end the boy remembers that it was Madame George herself who put him on the train, telling him, so flatly, as if she herself has to return him to whatever life it is he'll lead, "This is the train," him crying out to her, long after the train last left the city behind, then telling himself to say goodbye, *say goodbye goodbye goodbye goodbye goodbye goodbye goodbye goodbye, say goodbye, get on the train,* but always commanding himself to say it, saying it always to himself, never to Madame George, and because he cannot say the words out loud, she can't hear them, so he has to keep saying it, and in that way too the song doesn't end. Is it any wonder that people try to fix something so unfixed, so free of its own body as the Dick Slessig Combo's version of "Rock Your Baby" is free of "Rock Your Baby," that people have tried for more than forty years to contain it, to say exactly what it is, who it is, and what it isn't—which is to say whatever it might be to whoever might hear it? "I can remember to the day when I stopped teaching Virginia Woolf's *To the Lighthouse*," John Irving said in 1979. "I loved that little part called 'Time Passes.' . . . It's the difference between a novel of manners and a novel of *weight*, a novel of some kind of history, where it says, 'Hey look, "time changes."'"

I became so angry when I had to teach that book after Quentin Bell's biography came out. Not because the book is lousy. It *isn't*. But because the students were so willing to use that biography as an explanation for everything they read—and so many people read fiction that way it nauseates me.

It's difficult to tell people what the reason for that is without insulting them—because the real reason is that people with limited imaginations find it hard to imagine that anyone else has an imagination. Therefore, they must think that everything they read in some way *happened*. For years, I've sat with students, knowing full well that the worst, most *dreck-ridden* piece of their story is in the story because "That's just the way it happened." And I say, "Why is this dreadful scene, why is this stupid person here?" And the student says, "Oh, that's not a stupid person, that's my mother, and that's exactly what she said."

"They felt they had been *taken in*," Irving had said. But that's what art does—that's how it takes you somewhere else. And the phrase has its meanings. To be taken in means to be accepted into the brotherhood, the secret society, where all recognize the same signs. It means to be bereft, helpless, and then to be received off the street into a place where you will be cared for. It means to be fooled. And that is the bedrock meaning, the speech "Madame George" speaks: if you don't make the song happen to the person who knows nothing, who has never heard of your characters and has no reason to care about them, no matter how real they might be, the song didn't happen. And if you do make it happen, it did.

Josh Gleason, "Van Morrison: *Astral Weeks* Revisited," *Weekend Edition*, NPR, 28 February 2009.

Happy Traum, interview with Van Morrison, *Rolling Stone*, 9 July 1970, 33.

Jonathan Cott, "Bob Dylan," *Rolling Stone*, 26 January 1978, in *Bob Dylan: The Essential Interviews*, ed. Cott (Wenner Books, 2006), 187.

———"Van Morrison: The *Rolling Stone* Interview," *Rolling Stone*, 30 November 1978, 52.

"The original title was 'Madame Joy'": Ritchie Yorke, *Van Morrison: Into the Music* (London: Charisma, 1975), 60–61.

"It may have something to do": John Collis, *Inarticulate Speech of the Heart* (New York: Da Capo, 1996), 107.

Tom Nolan, "Who Was Madame George?" *Wall Street Journal* online, 14 April 2007.

Van Morrison and automatic writing, Jonathan Taplin, audio commentary, *The Last Waltz* DVD.

"John Irving: The *Rolling Stone* Interview," GM, *Rolling Stone*, 13 December 1979, 75, 71.

Mary Gaitskill, *Two Girls Fat and Thin* (New York: Poseidon, 1991), 225.

Marianne Faithfull, "Madame George," on *No Prima Donna: The Songs of Van Morrison* (Polydor, 1994). Produced by Van Morrison and Phil Coulter—whose theme music is all over *Breakfast on Pluto*.

Dick Slessig Combo—included as *Jessica Bronson and the Dick Slessig Combo present for your pleasure . . .* as part of the exhibition "Let's Entertain: Life's Guilty Pleasures" (Walker Art Center, Minneapolis; Portland Museum of Art, Portland, Oregon; Musée national d'art moderne, Paris [2000]; Museo Rufino Tamayo, Mexico City; and Miami Art Museum [2001]). From the exhibition catalogue (Minneapolis: Walker Art Center, 2000): "Working with Carl Bronson, [Jessica Bronson] has designed a curvilinear bandstand that is lit from below so that it appears to float in a pool of light. The band will perform on-stage on the opening night of the exhibition, leaving behind the lights and a looped compact disc of the performance for the duration of the exhibition. This empty stage with disembodied voices evokes notions of virtual pleasure and performance, the empty dreams of Hollywood, and the underbelly of spectacle. The machinery of fame—illumination, spectacle, performance—is laid bare, and the lack of a nice Hollywood ending suggests a disrupted narrative." Not to me—or, I think, the musicians. Other Dick Slessig Combo performances include versions of Kraftwerk's "Computer Love" and Bobby Gentry's "Ode to Billie Joe"; a 2004 single (dickslessig.com) was made up of a forty-two-minute dreaming-and-waking drift through Jimmy Webb's "Wichita Lineman" paired with a twenty-two-minute trudge through Crosby, Stills & Nash's "Guinnevere."

Van Morrison, "Madame George" (November 1967), plus "Goodbye George," "Dum Dum George," and other demo recordings (fall 1968), collected on *Payin' Dues* (Charly, 1994).

———"Madame George," *Astral Weeks* (Warner Bros.–Seven Arts, 1968).

SAINT DOMINIC'S PREVIEW. 1996

On the album of the same name, released in 1972, the year of Bloody Sunday in Derry, there was no escaping the immediacy of the song. Saint Dominic's Preview—was it a mass held for those who wouldn't see the next year? A special invitation-only pre-sale sale to empty Northern Ireland of everything it ever was before and was now ? For all that the phrase explained itself it might as well have been the Veedon Fleece, and that probably would have been in one of the sale bins if you knew how to look.

The cover of *Saint Dominic's Preview* featured a theatrical shot of Morrison sitting on what might have been church steps, holding a battered guitar. Save for an oddly dandyish kerchief around his neck his clothes were worn, with even a gaping hole in one pant leg, a street singer playing for coins and truth, his head slightly lifted toward the sky, his face sad but thoughtful, you could even say wistful, philosophical, his eyes gazing into the future, into the past: *Will this war never end?* You could buy a photocopied broadside called "The Troubles" off him for a dollar.

Even though Van Morrison has never written or sung a song with the phrase in it—no blues song, not even the cabaret blues "Trouble in Mind," planting the probably nineteenth-century southern verse "Sun gonna shine in my back door some day, wind gonna rise up, blow my blues away" in a twentieth-century New York penthouse—the portrait was as corny as it was contrived, and more fake. Morrison had worked for years to say nothing about the Troubles. The Sex Pistols might use the letters "IRA" in "Anarchy in the UK" like a bomb, but the acronym had never passed Morrison's lips in public, and for all one knows never will. In *In The Name of the Father*, Daniel Day-Lewis's Gerry Conlon is an out-of-control prankster IRA hanger-on in Belfast sent to London by his father because the IRA will kill him for his unreliability, then falsely imprisoned for an IRA London bombing. He has a poster on the wall of his cell to keep him alive, to affirm his innocence and his defiance: Johnny Rotten, not Van Morrison.

Whatever the intentions behind it, the cover of *Saint Dominic's Preview* worked as a setup, convicting the album's title song of falsity and bad faith—a song that in fact would name Belfast, and with a bitter regret weighting the word with all of its history, which is to say all of its killings—in advance. But the song was written and recorded before the cover was made, and it had fixed the game in advance: there was no false face it could not erase.

The song was stirring. It was exhilarating. The singer's commitment to his every word passed over to the listener even if the listener had never wasted a thought on Northern Ireland; there was a sense of engaging with the world on your own terms. As the scene shifted from Belfast to San Francisco to New York, shifted in phrases that barely made more narrative than a single word, as the story went from people being shot down in one street to people looking away from others as they walked down another to a rock 'n' roll singer at a party to promote his new album, what could have been felt as a slide from the profound to the trivial remained a story that stayed on its feet, that surrendered not a single measure of moral right from one side of the story to the other. When the song ended, you could feel you'd been around the world.

The specificity of the bare nod to Belfast went off like a gun. If, as more than one person has written, the title of Seamus Heaney's 1975 poem "Whatever You Say, Say Nothing" summed up both the aesthetic and the everyday life of avoidance in Northern Ireland in that time, when the cause writing your name on a bullet could as well be that of your presumed fellows as of your fated enemies, if not chance itself, could Morrison's work up to this moment have been a version of that poem itself, with "Whatever You Say, Say Nothing" boiled down, in the manner of a song, to nothing more than its phrase, sung over and over in endless variation? "Is there a link between that attitude, which Morrison seems to embody," a friend wrote, "and the yarragh? Can't we understand aspects of the yarragh as being at once a safe place beyond language"—when the wrong words could get you killed, or, with you safe at home in Marin County or New York or England, get someone who sang your song in the wrong place at the wrong time killed—"and an attempt to stretch for the sublime when the world, and Belfast is a world whether you're there in the flesh or not, is crowding you very tightly, and even a gut cry, a howl beyond words, is an embrace of the failure of language, a celebration of the faith that some things not only should not but can't be spoken of or even named?"

When Morrison performed the song on television twenty-four years later, the context was no longer clear. In 1972, the description of life in the Bay Area that Morrison offered in "Saint Dominic's Preview"—a utopia of sun, sloth, and solipsism, where nothing was more important than a refusal, in his words, to feel anybody else's pain, where the best struggled to get outside their empty shells, and failed—was so acute it wrote the script for a movie that wouldn't be shot for six years. Asked in 2000 why in 1978 he'd chosen to remake Don Siegel's 1956 *Invasion of the Body Snatchers*, and why he'd set it not in the film's original California Valley town but in San Francisco, Phil Kaufman, the director, didn't hesitate for a second: "I was living in San Francisco, it was the beginning of the New Age movement, and all I saw were pods." But in 1996 that was all a long time ago—even if the British torture of IRA militants, IRA bombs in London and UDA bombs in Belfast, each side executing not only the enemy but its own suspects, informers, collaborators, unreliables, anyone unlucky enough to have joined the right side at the wrong time, went on. For that matter, it had been awhile since a record company had put on a big bash for Van Morrison. The song had to make its own stage and raise its own curtain.

In 1996, the piece begins with a guitarist picking out a modal theme, a minor key that quickly loses itself in all that it might say: this could be the beginning of anything, a train song, a cowboy ballad, "Little Maggie." When Morrison begins to sing, about cleaning windows in Belfast, about Edith Piaf, a violin comes in, and the territory opens up—to San Francisco, then immediately across the country, in the old folk phrase "A long way to Buffalo," then across the ocean to Belfast again, and without your noticing the journey has turned strange, and the stakes have been raised. You can't tell when it was that Morrison began to push, when his voice lowered, when he began to play with the harsh vowels of his own gruff tone, when a hint of violence crept in—so that when he caught the history of a country as he pushed down with "Hoping that Joyce, don't blow the hoist," you realize you know exactly what he was talking about, even if time and place were now unfixed, even if you couldn't have explained "don't blow the hoist" to save your life.

The song went on, with horns, another guitar, maybe a mandolin, backing singers coming across with a quiet sympathy. The story went on. And yet, by the end—when the singer went from the record company party to an interview with a rock critic to another party in a fancy apartment on Fifty-Second Street—the shift in the song that in 1972 was lost in a mass finale, everyone playing at top volume, now came to the fore. After everything—after murder, after indifference, after flattery, after a no to all of it—everyone in the song turned to their windows, shocked, as perhaps they never were before, to see that the streets were now filled with people, people neither killing each other nor avoiding each other but marching as one, shouting for freedom, in the moment celebrating the truth that they already had it. Morrison looked out his window, surprised, confirmed, but most of all happy. "Can I get a witness!" he said, as if the words were no less a folk theme, part of the collective imagination, the common memory of anyone who might have already passed through the song, as Lead Belly testifying that "They was driving the women, just like the men" or Frank Hutchison promising "I won't be dead, just won't be here no more" when you came looking for him and he wasn't there.

Saint Dominic's Preview (Warner Bros., 1972).

"Saint Dominic's Preview" (1996) included on *SULT—Spirit of the Music* (Bottom Line/Koch, 1997) and on *Catalog Strays 1965–2000* (Wild Card bootleg).

SWEET THING. 1968

The music strides into its field like fate, and there are no obstacles: at the start, at the end of each phrase, the ping of a triangle marks the next step in the flight. It's the strangest thing—in this song, which I've never been able to play only once, that tiny moment can become the axis on which the whole piece turns. At first there's only Morrison's strum and Richard Davis's bass; as the arrangement takes full shape, as strings come in to take the measure that that ping once did, the chiming sound disappears. It's easy to forget—there's no triangle-player's wing in the Rock & Roll Hall of Fame. But when the song starts again, there it is, signaling a simplicity that the singer will soon leave behind. You can always re-cover it—you can even drag the song back and wait for the sound over and over again. You can't tell if the singer would even want to. Moving fast, he may have already forgotten the place in the song you don't want to leave.

After two and a half minutes, Davis seems to want to shut the song down. His bass makes a clacking sound, as if to put the brakes on the rhythm as everyone else rushes ahead; the brakes don't hold. *My my, my my, my mmm-my my, my my my*, Morrison muses; he takes a breath, and in one of the highest points in a song made of high points— "And I will run my merry way and jump the hedges first," is the first line; the image is so thrilling you never lose sight of it as the song moves on, and the singer never does stop jumping—he shifts into a higher gear. He finds an image that is as adult as the first is childlike, carrying specters the grown man cannot gainsay, an image that is less abandoned, more determined, but as much a sign of freedom, saying "And I will raise my hand up into the nighttime sky"—

> And I will raise my hand up into the nighttime . . .
> *skyyyyyyyyyy*

—and like the sound of the triangle, which is the song itself pausing for an instant to draw a breath, the moment of suspension is everything.

A minute later, Davis makes the same clacking sound again. This time he does take the reins of the music, and Morrison begins to drift away from the song. "Sweet thing," he says, as he's said throughout, but now that changes into "Sugar baby"—"Sugar baby, sugar baby," a phrase from before the blues, a phrase that helped shape it, a face hiding inside all the songs Morrison grew up loving, a phrase that

now belongs to him as much as it ever belonged to Lead
Belly or Dock Boggs.

Van Morrison, "Sweet Thing," *Astral Weeks* (Warner Bros.–Seven
    Arts, 1968).

TAKE ME BACK. 1991.
JENNIFER JASON LEIGH, 1995

Nostalgia pulls down like quicksand, and it's always had Van Morrison in its grip. He was twenty when he made "The Story of Them," about the band's days in Belfast at the Maritime Hotel, but the scene as he looked back was so perfect, the long-lost names and faces standing out so clearly through the haze of the intervening decades, or rather year, that he might have been eighty—even though, as he wrote and recorded the song, Them had yet to put out its second album. "Gotta walk away," he sang, tailing off, as if leaving the past behind was the same as building a palace for it.

All through his working life Morrison has fixed touchstones, talismans, charms—as if, from the time he was a boy, he saw the future as a forest, a wilderness of tangles and snares, and so like Hansel scattered crumbs that he might find his way back to a true home, except that his crumbs

166

were old Ray Charles records. As the years have gone on he
has turned ever more frequently to songs he treasured as a
boy—not for lack of his own songs, or even for fun or out of
affection, but as if to validate his own songs, anchor them, or
test the truth of his songs against songs that, the feeling must
be, can't lie. Even as his musical heroes have appeared in his
songs as characters—Ray Charles, Lead Belly, Jackie Wilson,
Billie Holiday, Sonny Boy Williamson, Charlie Parker, Sonny
Terry, Brownie McGhee, Mahalia Jackson, Elvis Presley, Fats
Domino, Lester Young, Lightnin' Hopkins, Jay McShann,
John Lee Hooker, Jerry Lee Lewis, Muddy Waters—he has
covered John Lee (the first Sonny Boy) Williamson's "Good
Morning Little Schoolgirl" and "Take Your Hand Out of My
Pocket" by Rice Miller, the second Sonny Boy Williamson,
Bobby Bland's "I'll Take Care of You," Waters's "I Just Want to
Make Love to You," Sam Cooke's "Bring It on Home to Me,"
Charles's "Lonely Avenue," "Georgia On My Mind," and "I
Can't Stop Loving You," but most often in a bland, passive
way, as if to take nothing from them. And that is to say noth-
ing of *How Long Has This Been Going On*, Morrison's 1996
album with Georgie Fame, filled with compositions by the
jump blues king Louis Jordan, King Pleasure and Lester
Young, Mose Allison, Harold Arlen and Johnny Mercer, and
Ira and George Gershwin's title song; from the same year, *Tell
Me Something*, an entire album of Mose Allison numbers;
You Win Again, his 2000 album with Lynda Gail Lewis,
shooting back and forth between covers of records by Hank
Williams, John Lee Hooker, Bo Diddley, Smiley Lewis, and
Jerry Lee Lewis; and, with *The Skiffle Sessions*, recorded at

Whitla Hall in Belfast in 1998, Morrison's reunion in spirit
and flesh with Lonnie Donegan, with Dr. John and longtime
British jazzman Chris Barber along for the ride, Lead Belly
everywhere: "Alabamy Bound," "Frankie and Johnny," "Good
Morning Blues," "Goodnight Irene," "Midnight Special."

Walking side by side in this never-ending stroll through
the bowers of days when all was cool, when the sound of
another voice, a young person's first apprehension of art,
could make it seem as if he and the world were one—when
the terrors of childhood and the alienations of adolescence
disappeared in that moment when you understood just how
Ray Charles pressed down so hard on the chorus of "Lonely
Avenue," and why—is the alienation that will not disappear:
the alienation from the world in which you have to live. It's
the cheats and liars and frauds and thieves and parasites and
writers and suck-ups and managers and promoters and
record companies and the people you called friends, all of
them, but more than anything it's the so-called modern
world, throwing itself in your face every day, so proud of itself, so sure of itself, so sure and proud that it has left the
past behind, and you with it, unless you're ready to play a
game you don't remotely comprehend.

It's no secret that when one reaches his or her forties,
maybe fifties, almost certainly his or her sixties and seventies, the world as it presents itself in advertisements, talk,
technology, dress, movies, music, money, and perhaps most
of all manners, the way in which people walk down the
street, the way they say hello or goodbye or don't bother to
do either, becomes an affront to one's entire existence. One
may reach a point, as the historian Robert Cantwell puts it

so gracefully, when one's "life begins to go into the past"—
that, or your whole fucking frame of reference.

Morrison has sung about the parasites in song after song,
from his whole string of demos in 1968 to "The Great De-
ception" in 1973, across the last twenty-five years in the likes
of "New Biography" (someone's written another book about
him), "A Town Called Paradise" ("copy cats stole" his words,
songs, melodies), the self-explanatory "Big Time Operators"
and "They Sold Me Out," and the no-one-listens-anyway
anthem "Why Must I Always Explain," which is a good song.
But he has sung far more powerfully about escape, about
running from the modern world, vanishing from it as if you
were never there. On *Hymns to the Silence*, a twenty-one song
set illustrated with photographs of grubby Belfast streets released in 1991, the theme was as ever-present as Lead Belly
on *The Skiffle Sessions*—or rather it was Lead Belly, Lead
Belly changed from flesh to idea. "I'm Not Feeling It Anymore," with "Have to get back," sung with bitter acceptance,
as if there's nothing left to feel; "On Hyndford Street," with
"Take me back, take me way, way, way back" the opening
for an entire catalogue of a teenager's discovery of the world,
reading "Mr. Jelly Roll" and "Mezz Mezrow's 'Really the
Blues,'" and "'Dharma Bums' by Jack Kerouac / Over and
over again." But none of that is really any preparation for
Morrison's nine minutes and eleven seconds of "Take Me
Back." Wait, wait, you could be forgiven for asking, didn't we
already hear that?

Morrison opens with a few seconds of harmonica so wistful you might be tempted to shut the song off right there, but
the pace is too slow, already too distant—the music is not

giving itself away. The harmonica continues to push, as if through fog. There's a sense of defeat. "Well, I remember," the singer says. "When life made more sense." Morrison will sing variations on this line ("Take me back, take me back, take me back, take me way, way, way back, way back, to when, when I understood") across the length of the song, and it's more painful every time. The singer has been forced to make this confession: to admit that the world no longer has a place for him, a place he may not deserve. He has made a wasteland, alluring, even beautiful, and dead; that is where the yarragh is in this song.

He drops down into a whisper, only a hint of piano and guitar behind him, and the music, now in a realm the modern world can't enter, a place of almost silence, ends without a marker, a note to tell you it has ended; it merely isn't there anymore. And it's as if you've fallen asleep for less than a second; nothing close to nine minutes seems to have passed.

But that was only the song's first life, and not its real life. That comes five years later, in the movie *Georgia*.

Released in 1995, the film pits Jennifer Jason Leigh's no-talent junkie punk singer Sadie against Mare Winningham's Georgia, Sadie's sister and a folk singer all but worshipped by her legions of fans. Georgia's voice—which is also that of Winningham, who has made her own albums—is all mellifluousness to Sadie's—Leigh's—horrid cracks and discords. The heart of the picture comes at a big AIDS benefit. Winningham appears to sing "Mercy," an uplifting ballad; her simple, modest "Hello" to the crowd brings a torrent of applause. "Mercy will you follow me," she sings, and the audience knows the answer: how could it resist? Then comes Sadie with nine drunken minutes of Morrison's "Take Me Back"—weirdly, exactly nine minutes and eleven seconds of "Take Me Back." Her seizing of the stage for an endless, no-range, flat, mindless assault on the defenseless song is presented in the film not as music but as a psychotic breakdown. It's meant to be as excruciating for the audience in the movie theater as for the people in the movie's concert hall; plainly, Sadie will keep singing until she or the song drops dead. Ultimately her sister appears on the stage like a fairy godmother, softly strumming her guitar, easing the madwoman off the stage.

Watching this car crash, you can't tell if this is the actor Leigh singing as Sadie or simply Leigh doing the best she can, and it doesn't matter. Sadie has nothing to bring to the song but the death wish that Morrison's song as he wrote it contains, something which, as Morrison recorded the song, is smothered by artistry, by a voice that cannot hide either the imagination inside of it or the command behind it. Leigh has nothing to bring to the song but will: no lift, no tone, no tricks. In Jonathan Lethem's phrase, she's an animal wandering through a karaoke machine, tangled in the gears and wires. All she can do is turn a concert hall into the street behind it where a junkie like her shows you her teeth as she asks for change, and then if you stop tries to tell you the story of her life. But she sings with the same up-and-down, back-and-forth refusal of time that women have always brought to songs, specifically work songs—and as the late musicologist Wilfred Mellers wrote of such music,* "Through repetition it carries the singers beyond the body's thrall. It at once affirms and transcends the physical, inducing a state of trance, even ecstasis, when the women begin to yell a magical 'music of the vowels,' which is beyond literate sequence and consequence."

What a remarkable thing to say: beyond consequence. But once the idea is there, you can hear Leigh travel beyond consequence—or rather, when the consequences of her performance arrive, they seem false, perhaps because Leigh's Sadie has touched the ecstasy Mellers calls down. Railing her takemebacks like someone hammering a single nail so many times she's now hammering through the wood, there are moments when the words come loose from themselves, and the singer is loosed from meaning, from purpose, from having to justify her existence to anyone at all—for seconds as the song grinds on, she is free. The song cracks open; a horde of beetles swarms out of it, and behind them all the naked, tortured men and women out of *The Garden of Earthly Delights*. Then Winningham's Georgia finally gets her sister to finish the song, to shut up. There's the barest ripple of clapping, no more than a sign of relief. Leigh—Sadie—immediately falls back into her crazy-pathetic persona, but in a way you don't want to believe, as if she's ashamed of

---

* Specifically "Robh thu 'sa' bheinn? (Were You in the Mountains?)," a Gaelic waulking song from the isle of Barra, off the coast of Scotland, sung by one "Mary Morrison and a group of old women": "They sing to aid their labour as they pound homemade cloth, 'waulking' it round in a sunwise direction against a board."

what she's done. "Thank you!" she says, her words smeared. "God bless! You're the real goods! Keep drinkin'—around the edges—I love you. I love you, Georgia," she says, sounding as if she's begging forgiveness for burning Georgia's doll collection in the fireplace when they were kids—and with the mere mention of Georgia's name there's lots of applause.

For nine minutes and eleven seconds, though, in a trance of terrible singing, Leigh has taken you right out of her not-very-good movie. While you were out, you were somewhere oddly quiet—a place that with "Take Me Back" Van Morrison marked on a map and Sadie the punk found.

Robert Cantwell, "Twigs of Folly" (1997, unpublished).

Wilfred Mellers, *A Darker Shade of Pale: A Backdrop to Bob Dylan* (New York: Oxford, 1985), 32, 33.

Jonathan Lethem, "The Fly in the Ointment," in *Best Music Writing 2009*, ed. GM (New York: Da Capo, 2009), 186.

Miss Mary Morrison and Calum Johnston, Kate Buchanan, and Flora Boyd, "Robh thu 'sa' bheinn?" on *Scottish Tradition 3: Waulking Songs from Barra* (School of Scottish Studies: University of Edinburgh, Greentrax, 1993, recorded 1965–1967). Earlier traditional recordings by Mary Morrison, made by Alan Lomax in 1951, can be heard, along with contemporaneous recordings by Penny Morrison, on *World Library of Folk and Primitive Music: Scotland* (Rounder, 1998).

Jennifer Jason Leigh, "Take Me Back," from *Georgia—Original Soundtrack* (Discovery, 1996). Also includes covers by Sadie's punk band, which includes Joe Doe of X, of the Velvet Underground's "There She Goes Again" (Doe) and "I'll Be Your Mirror" (Doe, Leigh, and Smokey Hormel), and of Lou Reed's

"Sally Can't Dance" (Doe and Leigh), plus, most startlingly, Stephen Foster's "Hard Times (Come Again No More)" by Mare Winningham (at the beginning, making you feel they never arrived) and by Leigh (at the very end, as if there'll never be anything else, and shouldn't be).

Them, "The Story of Them" (Decca, 1967, UK), included on *The Story of Them Featuring Van Morrison* (Polydor, 1998).

Van Morrison, "Take Me Back," *Hymns to the Silence* (Polydor, 1991).

————with Georgie Fame & Friends, *How Long Has This Been Going On* (Verve, 1996).

————*Tell Me Something: The Songs of Mose Allison* (Verve, 1996).

————and Linda Gail Lewis, *You Win Again* (Virgin, 2000). "Sometimes you make mistakes," Morrison said to Dave Marsh in 2009 when Marsh asked about the Fame and Allison and Lewis albums. "And sometimes you're bored."

————and Lonnie Donegan and Chris Barber, *The Skiffle Sessions—Live in Belfast 1998* (Virgin, 2000).

MYSTIC EYES. GREEK THEATRE, BERKELEY. 2009

At a concert where Morrison has played his way through all of *Astral Weeks*, surrounded by a four-person string section with a lead violinist, two drummers, guitarist Jay Berliner from the original sessions in 1968, an electric guitarist, a bass player alternating between bass guitar and bass fiddle, keyboard player (piano, organ, harpsichord), two female backup singers, a one-man horn section, a woman on acoustic guitar and steel guitar, with Morrison himself moving between alto sax, piano, acoustic guitar, harmonica—he finishes "Madame George," the last song of *Astral Weeks* as he will present it tonight, and floats into fragments of "Listen to the Lion," that long, speaking-in-tongues song from 1972. "All . . . my . . . love . . . comes tum-bling down," he chants. Suddenly it seems to be absolutely clear, the most obvious thing in the world, that from its first notes to its last *Astral Weeks* is nothing

more than a version of Wilson Pickett's "In the Midnight
Hour": "Not a song, but an epic," Jon Landau wrote in as
good a line as music writing has left behind. Nothing more,
and perhaps nothing less. I thought of the film of Roddy
Doyle's novel *The Commitments*, the story of a teenage
Dublin soul band, taking their stand in the late 1980s, when
nobody knows and nobody cares, but the Commitments will
make them care. (Morrison himself was solicited for the role
of Joey "The Lips" Fagan, an old trumpeter the kids bring in
to have someone to look up to, some link to a past they can
create but not remember.)* Now it's the night of their big
show, Wilson Pickett himself is in town, they do everything
they can to get him to come to their show, to bless them with
his presence, to give them a face to look into that they will
never forget as surely as Wilson Pickett will forget theirs. The
show ends; he isn't there. But it was a great show. The boys
and girls in the Commitments justified their existence—their
existence on earth, not merely their momentary existence as
a soul band. And as they scatter, as they raise their glasses, the
film finds Mr. Pickett—no actor, the man himself. His own
show is done; tells his limo driver to take him to this other

---

* The movie was directed by Alan Parker and produced by Lynda Myles,
who, when in 2009 I asked about Morrison's involvement, wrote: "VM
came over to see Alan and met in Alan's hotel room in London. He arrived with his manager, having been sent pages of the script in advance.
The manager said that VM required a club sandwich. There was no
small talk while this was delivered and VM ate the sandwich. The manager kept saying how keen VM was to be in the movie. Van continued to
eat the sandwich. He was asked to read but refused. When Alan asked
why not, VM said 'because it's shit.' The meeting was then basically
abandoned."

show, this band, what are they called? Of course he'd sung "In the Midnight Hour" that night. Where else would Van Morrison have first heard *Astral Weeks*?

The thought passed in an instant as Morrison sang "And my love comes tumbling down" one more time, now no distance at all between that and Pickett's deliberate, unstoppable pledge:

> I'm going to wait til the midnight hour
> That's when my love comes tumbling down

It was the sort of reverie that comes at those times in a show when in the audience you feel as if you are seeing all around the event as it happens, the past not past at all, more voices than those on the stage singing the song. Then Morrison raised his harmonica, as if to ornament his words, and flew like his own missile into "Mystic Eyes." It was shocking, blood in the sylvan glade, the headless horseman in the Kentucky Derby riding the wrong way, and it lasted only long enough for it to be uncertain if it had happened at all.

Roddy Doyle, *The Commitments* (Dublin: King Farouk, 1987; New York: Vintage, 1989).

The Commitments, dir. Alan Parker (1991, DVD 1999, 20th Century Fox). Johnny Murphy played Joey "The Lips" Fagan.

Wilson Pickett, "In the Midnight Hour" (Atlantic, 1965).

BEHIND THE RITUAL. 2008

"Don't need no juice to unwind," Van Morrison says in "Don't Go to Nightclubs Anymore," early on on *Keep It Simple*, his last album of new songs to be released as I write. Then he says the same thing in different ways three more times. *Go ahead, knock this bottle off my shoulder!* But the only song on *Keep It Simple* that makes its own time and place is anything but simple.

"Behind the Ritual"—you could make up a picture of Morrison as Michelangelo's Adam holding out his hand to God's, with the opposite of Adam's cool gaze on his face, and get away with using it for the cover of a third of all the albums he's ever made. The religious yearning in his music that first surfaced explicitly in "Astral Weeks" has been a constant ever since, like references to backstreet jelly roll or gardens all wet with rain. It can be as airborne as it is on "Full Force Gale" in 1979—when Morrison says, "I've been lifted up again / By the Lord," Toni Marcus's fiddle can make it feel as if you've been lifted high enough to at least glimpse what the singer is seeing—or as entombed as it is all over *Avalon Sunset* ten years later, an album that leads off with a duet with the 1950s British rock 'n' roll pioneer and noted evangelical Cliff Richard. It smothered Morrison's voice for nearly two decades. But here it's never clear what the ritual is or what it promises.

"Behind the Ritual" takes seven minutes to end the album—to inhale it like smoke and make it disappear. It starts with Morrison strumming a ukulele and the drummer moving slowly from a woodblock to traps. The words are slurred, or maybe it's that the old man singing them is singing them as clearly as he can, testing his tongue against his pursed lips, like someone whose fingers are so webbed with arthritis he has to draw words instead of writing them. Morrison lifts his saxophone, and gets the lucidity he can't find on his own.

It all burns off like fog. He's taken you into an alley, the same alley, he seems to be saying, where Uncle John met Long Tall Sally, but also a place where boys just into their teens once gathered to do all the things the stolid singer in "Don't Go to Nightclubs Anymore" says he doesn't do, doesn't want, doesn't need: drinking, smoking, bragging about girls they haven't touched and the snappers they're going to give them, talking jive, saying *fuck* and *shit* when someone mentions church. Now that stolidity—the granite face on the front of the album that has "Behind the Ritual" on it—has been replaced by desire, and desire bleeds all

over the music. "Given the courage, we live by moments of
interference between past and present, moments in which
time comes back into phase with itself," the historian Roger
Shattuck wrote in 1958. "It is the only meaning of history.
We search the past not for other creatures but for our own
lost selves."

It is the deepest nostalgia, where some things you did,
some things you saw, and some things you heard about
replace any sense of life as it is, its true burdens, struggles,
paradox, failures, betrayals. You can argue against the idea,
but you can't argue against music if it moves you, you can
only listen or change the station or turn off the radio and
say you don't do that sort of thing anymore. But you can
also get the feeling, as Morrison leads his old self back into
the alley, sits down with the boys, drinks their wine, offers
them his, whispering, because what they do is secret, not
the act so much as the warmth of friendship and of the forbidden that the act leaves in the air like perfume, that *this* is
the mystic, this is the astral plane, nothing given by God or
located in another dimension, but memory, true or false.

It's true if the singer can make it true. Morrison circles the
words like faces that are slipping their names, bits of tunes
that won't let you sing them. He circles the people he finds in
the alley in the same way, talking them into being. What he's
summoning is all in the past, but you can sense that the
drama has yet to play itself out. It's an adventure, and no
one knows, no one could understand. "We few, we happy few,
we band of brothers," says one of the boys out of *Henry V*,
and Morrison answers him out of *Julius Caesar*: "How many

ages hence / Shall our lofty scene be acted over / In states un-
born and accents yet unknown?"

The theme takes shape in steps. There is drinking in the
alley, there's making time with Sally, there's dancing drunk
in the alley, there's making up rhymes in the alley, there's
turning and spinning in the night, verse after verse, each
one a slight variation, a tiny step past the one before it.
From the old man sharing a secret there's another man, perhaps no less old but stronger, less afraid of himself, singing
as if hoping someone outside of the alley will hear him, or
to make certain the buildings rising up from the alley hear
him and never forget. But he also wants to explain. It's all
one quest: behind the ritual, he says, you find the spiritual.

"Behind the ritual" now become the key words on which
all other words turn, around which all the rhythms of the
song will shape themselves. And as always in Van Morrison's
highest moments, the words come loose from their own
song and remake it, leading the singer down their own path.
"The only time I actually work with words is when I'm writing a song. After it's written, I release the words"—and now
the words circle the song and choose the words they want to
marry. At one point, as if to free the words from their own
bodies, to divest them of any chance to signify, to let the
word begin again in sound and find its own way out, Morrison throws away them all—

> Blah blah blah blah blah blah
> Blah blah blah blah blah blah
> Blah blah blah blah blah blah

Blah blah blah blah blah blah
Blah blah blah blah blah blah

—but it doesn't work, and it doesn't work because it isn't
needed. By now the words themselves are rituals. The
words are already free, and immediately as they regain their
form they cast their spell again: *Getting hiiiiiiiiiiiiigh, behind the ritual, so high—behind the ritual.*

Behaaaaaand the ritual, the singer twisting the word,
making it gnarled and threatening—behind the ritual, the
singer wanted to tell you, is the spiritual, but now the ritual,
gathering every Saturday night in the alley with a bottle of
sweet wine, is the spiritual, and the spiritual, that state of
grace, is this tawdry ritual. The words begin to come apart,
away from the transcendent, from that sense that there is always something unknown, a revelation that will leave you
changed, behind the holiest rituals: isn't that what the church
is for? No, it's life and what you want from it between the
time you wake and the time you sleep.

The song pulls the singer farther and farther away from
the truths it's rightfully his duty to tell you, the lessons you
can learn from his mistakes, the peace of mind that is his and
can be yours. But the voice is so expressive, so contained
within itself and capable of going anywhere: "this music," the
director and one-time rock critic Wim Wenders wrote about
Morrison in 1970, "gives you a feeling and a notion of what
films could be like: *perception* that doesn't always jump
blindly at meanings and assertions, but rather lets your
senses extend further and further."

You never do get out of the alley with this song. You never get back to the rest of the album, or for that matter to the rest of Morrison's career. It could stop right here. But over the course of that career one might have said the same thing a dozen times.

Roger Shattuck, *The Banquet Years: The Origins of the Avant-Garde in France, 1885 to World War I* (1958; rev. ed. New York: Vintage, 1968).

"The only time": Jonathan Cott, "Van Morrison: The *Rolling Stone* Interview," *Rolling Stone*, 30 November 1978, 52.

Wim Wenders, "Van Morrison," *Filmkritik*, June 1970, collected in *Emotion Pictures* (London: Faber and Faber, 1989), 53–54.

Van Morrison, "Behind the Ritual," on *Keep It Simple* (Lost Highway, 2008).

ACKNOWLEDGMENTS

My thanks go to Dave Marsh, William, Paula, and Erik Bernstein, Jon Landau, Jonathan Cott, Ben Schafer of Da Capo, Clinton Heylin, the indefatigable Toby Gleason, Danielle Madeira of Another Planet, Joel Selvin, Josh Gleason, John Elrod, Lynda Myles, Marc Smirnoff, Devin McKinney, Scott Foundas, David Patton, and the gracious and forthcoming Michael Sigman; to Jann Wenner at *Rolling Stone*, Marvin Garson and the late Sandy Darlington at the San Francisco *Express-Times*, the late Lester Bangs and the late Barry Kramer at *Creem*, Jon Carroll, Bill Broyles, and Nancy Duckworth at *New West*, David Frankel at *Artforum*, Bill Wyman at *Salon*, Graham Fuller at *Interview*, Alice O'Keefe at the *New Statesman*, and Jeffrey M. Perl of *Common Knowledge*; and to Emily, Cecily, Steve Perry, and Jenny, for the night at the Avalon Ballroom where this book first took shape.

INDEX

ff

Faber and Faber is one of the great independent publishing houses. We were established in 1929 by Geoffrey Faber with T. S. Eliot as one of our first editors. We are proud to publish award-winning fiction and non-fiction, as well as an unrivalled list of poets and playwrights. Among our list of writers we have five Booker Prize winners and twelve Nobel Laureates, and we continue to seek out the most exciting and innovative writers at work today.

Find out more about our authors and books
faber.co.uk

Read our blog for insight and opinion on books and the arts
thethoughtfox.co.uk

Follow news and conversation
twitter.com/faberbooks

Watch readings and interviews
youtube.com/faberandfaber

Connect with other readers
facebook.com/faberandfaber

Explore our archive
flickr.com/faberandfaber